Staying on Top and

Keeping the Sand Out of Your Pants

STAYING ON TOP AND KEEPING THE SAND OUT OF YOUR PANTS

A Surfer's Guide to the Good Life

WHY LET LIFE WIPE YOU OUT WHEN YOU CAN SURF TO SUCCESS?

Scott Miller, Mark A. Hubble and Seth Houdeshell

With Cartoons by John Byrne

Health Communications, Inc.
Deerfield Beach, Florida

www.hcibooks.com

Library of Congress Cataloging-in-Publication Data

Miller, Scott D.
    Staying on top and keeping the sand out of your pants : a surfer's guide to the good life / Scott Miller, Mark A. Hubble, and Seth Houdeshell.
      p. cm.
    Includes bibliographical references.
    ISBN 0-7573-0033-2 (pbk.)
    1. Success—Psychological aspects.   2. Self-actualization (Psychology)   I. Hubble, Mark A., date.   II. Houdeshell, Seth, date. III. Title.

BF637.S8M565 2003
158.1—dc21

                               2003041734

HCI, its Logos and Marks are trademarks of Health Communications, Inc.

Publisher: Health Communications, Inc.
          3201 S.W. 15th Street
          Deerfield Beach, FL 33442-8190

Authors may be contacted for information and presentations at *info@talkingcure.com*.

A portion of the proceeds from the sale of this book will be donated to the Surfrider Foundation. The Surfrider Foundation is a nonprofit environmental organization dedicated to the protection and enjoyment of the world's oceans, waves and beaches for all people through conservation, activism, research and education. For more information, contact 800-743-SURF or visit *www.surfrider.org*.

Cover illustration by John Byrne
Cover design by Peter Quintal
Inside book design by Dawn Von Strolley Grove

Live all you can . . . the right time is *any* time. . . .

Henry James

Contents

Surfz Up Now!
Get Your Board and
Get to the Beach

It's time to start
living the life we've imagined.

Henry James

So, you want the good life, eh? Of course, who wouldn't? People have been chasing after it in some form or another as long as there have been people on the planet. Here's the good news: *It's available right now.* That's right. There's no special line to wait in, no pill to take, no guru to follow, no workshop to attend nor self-help book to study. It's true. You don't need a promotion at work or any more money than you have in your pocket. Neither do you need tighter abs, bigger breasts or any more hair on your head than

your genes are going to provide. And no, you don't have to wait until you're smarter, finished with your therapy or MBA, amassed more self-esteem, or brought out and diapered your inner child. In short, *there is nothing to prepare for.* To paraphrase the Chinese philosopher Confucius from nearly three thousand years ago, "The door is open. Why is it that no one enters?" Or as surfers worldwide say today, "Surfz up, dude! Get your board and get to the beach."

We know, we know. Right now, you're thinking, *Wait a minute. Are these guys kidding? Surfers? Confucius maybe—after all, anything that smacks of Zen is kind of in fashion right now. But, come on, surfers? Here I draw the line. What could those board-toting, baggy-panted, perpetual adolescents possibly know about the "good life"?* To this, we say, "Hey, we *resemble* that remark!" That's right, we're surfers. And while each of us differs in age, haircut and preferred style of surfing, we've all found that it offers a *vision* for seeing and experiencing the opportunities breaking on the shores of life. So whether you're an individual trying to paddle out of the doldrums or the CEO of a company

pummeled by the waves of the competition, this book aims to help you stay on top and keep the sand out of your pants.

Okay, so *why* surfing? Because, to the surfer, the world is an ocean of opportunity, an endless shoreline of possibilities served up free of charge through no effort of one's own. All a surfer has to do to take advantage of what's available is pick up a board and get to the beach.

For all the people living away from the coast, you may say, "I'm landlocked! What beach? Get outta here!" We hear that, but location is no excuse. Consider this: Surfers trek through an area known as Deadman's Forest, past brown bears foraging for food along the banks of Deadman's River, just to take advantage of the opportunity to surf in the balmy thirty-two-degree waters off the *Alaskan* coast.

How 'bout bad weather? No problem, as the surf is always bound to be up somewhere else. Plus, being stormed out one day simply means the waves will be bigger the next.

Poor surf? Surfers say, "Dude, it's not the size of the wave but

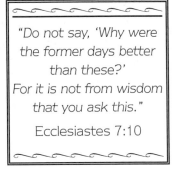

"Do not say, 'Why were the former days better than these?'
For it is not from wisdom that you ask this."

Ecclesiastes 7:10

the motion of the ocean." So stop reminiscing about yesterday's waves or dreaming about tomorrow's. You can't ride those waves anyway. Just get your board and get to the beach.

Maybe you're worried about wiping out. Here's a thought: The 1963 song "Wipe Out" by the Surfaris went to number two on the *Billboard* charts, making it the highest-ranking surfing instrumental ever. If getting munched was really that bad, you have to wonder why anyone would write such a cool song about it and why surfers would still be singing its praises four decades later. Maybe that's why surfers refer to the best waves as "death." Bottom line? Everyone goes through the "rinse cycle" now and then—it's part of catching waves, so get over it.

Think you're too old? Consider this: If a dog named Koda can become a celebrity by learning to ride the waves off Bolinas, California, then any old dog can learn new tricks. A recent story on National Public Radio recounted the surfing career of several newcomers to the sport. Get this: The youngest was fifty-nine and the oldest eighty-nine years old! No Depend®s here—they grabbed their boards and got to the beach.

Surfers say: Don't settle in as you age; break out. And if you're just breaking out, great. After you've been on top of your first wave, you'll be stoked for more. You'll also be tempted to kick yourself for all the opportunities that passed you by unnoticed—but don't waste your time *unless* you're kicking yourself all the way to the nearest beach. New waves are breaking right now. Pick up your board and get rolling.

Finally, no board? No problem. You can always body*surf.* As the old expression goes, "Whatever floats your boat." Sadly, it's easy to get tricked into thinking that to enjoy a more rewarding or "good life," you must first *have* this or that (e.g., better duds, better board, better wheels, better waves, better weather, better tan), or *do* or *accomplish* something

> "*Most people spend most of their days doing what they do not want to do in order to earn the right, at times, to do what they most desire.*"
>
> John Mason Brown

(e.g., earn more money, get a degree, invent something new, discover something or be discovered). It is as though somewhere along the way, society changed the old Boy Scout motto from "Be prepared" to

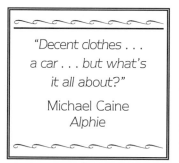

"Decent clothes . . . a car . . . but what's it all about?"

Michael Caine
Alphie

"Always be preparing." Things are never good enough; there's always something left to do.

You don't need a degree in sociology to notice that Americans are in a constant state of upgrading, retooling, remodeling, reengineering, reclothing and remaking. The result is that America has become the land of big houses, big cars, big debt and big butts (a staggering 64.5 percent of adult Americans are overweight).[1]

A recent TV commercial is a perfect example of how the "good life" has become conflated with how much one produces and, more importantly, spends and consumes. An attractive young couple is shown climbing a sheer cliff on a beautiful sunny day. What do they do once they reach the top of the escarpment? Enjoy the view? Each other? No, these Madison Avenue representations of the "good life" whip out their shiny new laptops and get straight to work.

Or consider what has happened to the family vacation. Gone is any hope of relaxation. In its place is the obligatory *adventure.* By the time the odyssey is over, Mom and Dad are exhausted, the kids are cranky, and the bill adds up to the national debt. Worse yet is the oxymoronic "working vacation" where cell phones and

POP'S WORKING VACATION JUST ISN'T WORKING..

---

[1] Hellmich, N., "Obesity in America Is Worse than Ever." *USA Today,* October 9, 2002. p.1.

e-mail have replaced "getting away from it all" with "staying in touch."

Surfers say: negatory. Think this way and you'll die waiting for the "good life." Along the way, you'll also go broke chasing after fads and fashions or paying experts to save you from the lack of fulfillment and meaning in your life. Maybe this is why credit-card debt and bankruptcies are at an all-time high while people's ratings of happiness and sense of personal fulfillment are at record lows.

Simply put, we've confused *having* (feelings, experiences, stuff) with *living* the good life. In this vein, there's a story about a thief who breaks into the beach house of a wise old surfer known as Surfmaster, only to discover there isn't much to steal. "You have come a long way to visit," the surfer says to the thief, "and should not return empty-handed. Please take my surfboard and clothes as a gift." The thief is surprised but slinks away with the clothes and board in hand. Afterwards, the seasoned old surfer sits naked watching the waves breaking on the beach. *Poor fellow,* he thinks, *I wish I could give him these bodacious waves.* As Surfmaster knows, it's not possible to buy, beg, borrow or steal the good life. It has to be lived.

By the way, don't despair if the only surfing you've done lately is

the channels on your TV set. The hurry-up, work-harder, pack-more-in pace of today's world has a quality similar to being stuck in and tossed about by the foam churning at the shoreline. Bombarded by numerous demands on our time, energy and attention, the average person is barely able to catch a breath before being sucked back out by the undertow of life for another thrashing. Experts tell us we have "attention deficit disorder." In our experience, we suffer from attention fatigue.

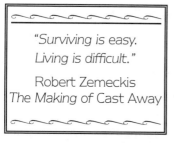

"Surviving is easy.
Living is difficult."

Robert Zemeckis
The Making of Cast Away

Like inexperienced swimmers, we often make matters worse by fighting *against* the current rather than giving in and flowing leisurely back out to where opportunities for a ride are on the rise. Worn out from the constant activity, most of us are relieved when we finally manage to struggle out of the surf or are washed up on shore away from the action. Then, wrapped in the warmth of a beach towel, we either rest for a short time before rushing pell-mell back into the fray or emerge from our cotton cocoon content to watch the action from the safety of the nearest beach chair.

We know personally just how easy it is to get stuck in the foam, to be frenetically busy, have all the trappings of involvement, think you're being productive and getting things done, and yet feel strangely removed from life at the end of the day. It would be gratifying to say that we quickly assessed the problem and managed to free ourselves. The truth is, the nagging feeling that something was missing only led us to thrash about and paddle ever *more* wildly—much as a drowning swimmer. No matter how much we floundered, we held on to the belief that our hard work and dedication would eventually propel us to the top—the Atlantis of our ambitions, the heaven of our hopes, in other words, the "good life."

It didn't work, of course. We just ended up tired and exhausted, feeling more washed up than on top of life. By the way,

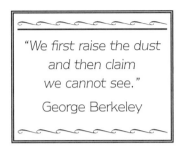

"We first raise the dust and then claim we cannot see."

George Berkeley

this reminds us of another story: A man stands out in front of his home every morning and swings his dog around by the tail for several minutes. When a neighbor asks why the man treats the dog so cruelly, he replies, "Why, you have no idea how happy the dog is when I stop." We were that dog!

Rest or no rest, at that point we had absolutely no desire to run back into the froth and foam. If nothing else, we'd learned not to mistake frantic activity for forward motion. At the same time, we weren't willing to throw down our towels alongside all the other tourists who, confusing entertainment with opportunity, seem content with whatever the culture dishes up as fulfillment. We were better than that. We'd been to college. We had advanced degrees. We were *gifted* for heaven's sake. But what were we to do?

Faced with either drowning or settling, we chose, in a manner of speaking, to pack up our lives and leave the beach altogether. Not ones to fill the resulting void with alcohol, drugs or the latest pharmaceutical wonder, we got high on grumbling, faultfinding and poking fun at everything and everyone. Over time, however, the escalating outrage needed to feed our growing habit only compounded our feelings of disaffection and dissatisfaction. In effect, we became grumpy young men.

The people around us—our families and friends—couldn't

fathom why we were so grouchy and unhappy. "Look at everything you have going for you," they would say. "You've got so much to be grateful for." And they were right. We had good jobs, nice families, lived in first-rate neighborhoods and had more than our share of leisure time. In fact, we had what 99 percent of the world's population associates with the "good life." So what was the matter with us? Why didn't we get it?

One day, a surfer is caught in an unexpected storm and carried away. After floating aimlessly for a number of days, he washes up on the shore of a deserted island. Initially, the surfer tends to his wounds and survives by eating the sweet and abundant tropical fruits growing nearby. Determined not to spend the rest of his life marooned, he soon begins constructing a raft out of fallen palm trees and the remnants of his old surfboard. To build his strength for the journey, he also sets out to capture and eat a small pig that shares the island with him. This is easier said than done. No matter what the stranded surfer tries, the creature always manages to elude capture. The chase continues and intensifies. Each day, he spends more time and precious energy running after the pig. Each day brings renewed failure.

The pursuit goes on for months until sailors from a passing ship

land on the remote island. While picking fruit, they discover the surfer lying face down in the sand, weak and emaciated. "He's alive," one of the seamen shouts after feeling for a pulse. "Bring water," says another and then, lifting the surfer to a sitting position, asks, "Can we help you, mate?" Slowly lifting a bony finger and pointing off in the distance, the surfer replies, "You sure can . . . *you see that pig over there . . . ?*"

So what was the matter with us? Why didn't we get it? Like the surfer in the story, we failed to see the opportunities right before our eyes. They were there. They'd been happening all along. Seeing them, however, required making a choice. It was that simple. Were we going to be surfers or remain wannabes?

Just so we're clear, this is not

> *"When one door of happiness closes, another opens; but often we look so long at the closed door that we do not see the one which has been opened for us."*
>
> Helen Keller
> *We Believed*

about adopting an optimistic, everything-works-out-for-the-best, make-lemonade-out-of-lemons outlook. Indeed, we personally found all of that you-can-help-yourself, self-help stuff useless. Why? Because by helping us cope, it functioned more like a life preserver than a kickboard. Sure, we stayed afloat, but in the same place. The surfer in the story, for example, did not need to read a book about how to catch pigs, attend a support group for frustrated pig catchers or overcome his "meat issues." Rather, he needed to take advantage of the opportunity before him. It was a choice.

If *you* are ready to make that choice now, then turn the page.

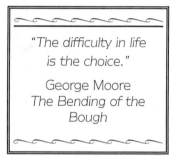

"*The difficulty in life is the choice.*"

George Moore
The Bending of the Bough

Surfer or Wannabe: Which Will You Be?

Surfer \sûr´fᵊr \ n [origin unknown] (1) Someone who rides the crests of waves as they are breaking; (2) someone who is able to scan a wide range of offerings for something that is interesting or fills a need; (3) someone able to take advantage of the opportunities at hand. *No synonyms available. Antonym:* wannabe.

Wannabe \wŏn´ᵃ-bē \ n [condensation of the phrase want-to-be] (1) Someone who imitates the behavior, customs or dress of an admired person or group; (2) a would-be (imitation) surfer. *See also* tourist, poser, wish was, shore rat and foam rider. *Antonym:* surfer.

S o, which will you be, a surfer or a wannabe? Sounds like a no-brainer, doesn't it? Truth is, while the choice may be simple, it is not *easy*. In fact, it is so hard to make this simple, life-transforming choice that you often only hear about it after people narrowly escape death, or lose a family member or close friend. Folks may also confront this defining moment when they are downsized at work, hear the loud tick of their own biological clock or learn they're to be parents for the first time. How is it that we are loath to change unless faced with our own mortality? Simply put, because life is otherwise *bearable*—and that's the real trap.

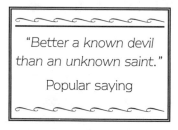

"Better a known devil than an unknown saint."

Popular saying

Let's look at this dilemma through the eyes of a surfer. It's no accident that most people who visit the seashore choose to lay around or play on the beach or hang out in the shallow waters near the shoreline. First of all, it seems like there's a lot to do. You can cool off in the water, build sandcastles, check out the beach babes and dudes, or drink beer and eat hot dogs. If you get bored, you can stroll along the boardwalk or read the latest summer blockbuster. Aside from the occasional sunburn, it's remarkably safe. There are no jellyfish or sharks to worry about and little chance of drowning. Plus, if you do end up in trouble, there are plenty of people around—including lifeguards—to give you a hand. It feels idyllic. Unless the weather takes a dramatic turn for the worse, a storm blows in or a boatload of hazardous waste is dumped nearby, why would anyone leave? Surfers say, "Because there are no waves there." Plus, hang out there long enough and you'll invariably end up with sand in your pants—nothing fatal or unbearable, just irritating.

What's a wannabe to do? How do you change from shore sitter or foam rider to surfer? To start, loosen your grip on that hot dog you've been munching. Next, peel your fingers off that beer and your eyes away from that perfect ten in the thong or guy in the form-fitting spandex bikini

> "The only thing which consoles us for our miseries is diversion, and yet this is the greatest of our miseries."
>
> Blaise Pascal

bathing suit. And finally, lift your eyes and look out to sea.

Beyond the froth and foam, the huddled masses on the beach "yearning to breathe free," what *do* you notice? There, rising and falling, always in motion, rolling left, then right, then back again, extending as far as the eye can see, all the way to the horizon and beyond, is the ocean. Three hundred plus million cubic miles of water covering more than 70 percent of the Earth's surface, the majority of which remains unexplored and totally unknown to humankind. The ocean is the undisputed source of life on our planet, containing 97 percent of the world's higher-order species and having the same salinity as human blood. It is a massive, unrelenting and

unstoppable force, unequaled by any other on the planet.

If you make your way through the crowds and swim out *beyond* the sloppy soup at the shoreline, you'll not only see, but also *feel* that power. In the water, the law of gravity bows to the will of the ocean and is temporarily suspended. Through no effort of your own, you are first lifted and then quickly and gently returned

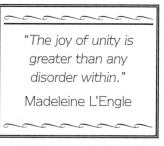

"*The joy of unity is greater than any disorder within.*"

Madeleine L'Engle

to your feet. Up. Then down. First elevated. Then grounded. Far from making you vulnerable, *giving in* to the undulating rhythm offers the chance of connection with something greater than yourself. Indeed, becoming a part of the ongoing set of opportunities from one swell to the next is precisely what surfers know and find appealing about the ocean.

"*To see things as they are, the eyes must be opened; to see things as other than they are, they must open even wider; to see things as better than they are, they must be open to the full.*"

Antonio Machado
Juan de Mairena

As surfers do every day, you can move in and be part of it, or you can step out of it. *It's your choice.* Just open your eyes as wide as possible. Look beyond the hustle and bustle at the shoreline of your everyday life to where the waves are forming and breaking. And then, *step into* the surf.

History is replete with stories of people who acquired the "good life" by choosing to step into the surf, seeing and connecting with the opportunities in the world

around them. For example, in the spring of 1891 the twenty-nine-year-old son of a soap manufacturer moved from Philadelphia to Chicago with little more than thirty-two dollars and a strong ambition to start his own soap-selling business. To gain new customers, the young man offered merchants incentives to buy his brand of soap instead of more established products. One of the inducements he offered was a can of baking powder. No kidding! This was long before prepackaged cake mixes became widely available and even longer before people bought most of their baked goods already prepared.

The wannabe soap salesman soon noticed that the baking powder was a more popular item than his soap. Seizing the opportunity, the young man jettisoned his soap business and began selling baking powder. Within a year, he changed his entire business again after noticing that the chewing gum he offered with each can of baking powder was more popular than the powder itself. That

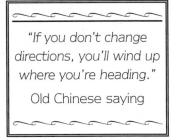

"If you don't change directions, you'll wind up where you're heading."

Old Chinese saying

young entrepreneur was William Wrigley Jr., founder of the Wrigley Chewing Gum Company. You know, the manufacturer of Spearmint, Juicy Fruit, Doublemint, Freedent, Big Red and Extra.

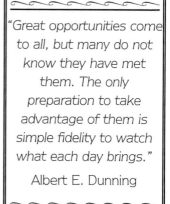

To be sure, William Wrigley could have wiped out at any number of points along the way. For example, he could have stayed put in Philadelphia, choosing to work comfortably in his father's business rather than venturing out on his own into uncharted waters.

Once in Chicago, he could have thrashed about in the foam and froth of the soap business instead of catching the rising baking-powder wave. After all, it's not like he wasn't selling any soap at all. He wasn't starving, nor was he living on the streets. Besides, he had his pride and heritage to consider—he was the son of a soap manufacturer! And what did he know about chewing gum, anyway?

> *"Great opportunities come to all, but many do not know they have met them. The only preparation to take advantage of them is simple fidelity to watch what each day brings."*
>
> Albert E. Dunning

For all that, Wrigley was not weighed down by any of these considerations. More importantly, he didn't create the waves he eventually rode to success; he simply noticed and then got onboard the opportunities as they arose. Like a surfer, he kept his eyes wide open, scanning the vast ocean of possibilities for incoming waves.

Now, you may be thinking, *That's okay for Wrigley, but I'm not selling soap, and I don't chew gum. So what in the heck does this have to do with me and my (insert your own story here [boring job, meaningless life, tolerable marriage, knuckleheaded family, etc.])?* To this, we say, you're right. You're absolutely right. But as the wise old Surfmaster says, "When my finger points at a wave, don't look at my finger because you'll miss the wave." Of course, it's not about gum, baking powder or soap. It's about *consciously* and *actively* putting yourself in the right place at the right time. It's the full-body version of opening your eyes.

There's no mystery to this process. Take a lesson from surfers. They listen to the morning surf report on the radio, log onto the Web to check out the breakers via webcam, talk with locals and swap stories with their buds. In short, they're always on the lookout for waves.

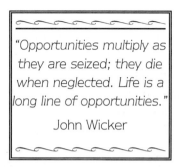

> *"Opportunities multiply as they are seized; they die when neglected. Life is a long line of opportunities."*
>
> John Wicker

There are a zillion stories illustrating this idea. In fact, true to the point we're making, the more we opened our eyes, the more stories we found. Consider Maeve Binchy. The bestselling author of three volumes of short stories, two plays, an award-winning teleplay and twelve novels didn't publish her first book until she was forty-three years of age. Where did the inspiration come from for that first novel? Binchy heard two women gossiping on a bus and thought, *That would make an interesting story.*

In truth, Binchy was no novice when it came to spotting opportunities. Years earlier, when working as a schoolteacher, she'd taken some time off to tour Israel. Her father was so impressed with the letters she wrote home about the war-torn country that he sent one to the *Irish Times.* When the leading daily paper offered to pay more for that letter than she was making as a teacher, Binchy took up writing. Actually, she became an editor at the *Times!*

How about the Springfield, Massachusetts, lithographer who'd been doing a brisk business with his new picture of Abraham Lincoln until the presidential candidate suddenly decided to grow a beard? When sales of the picture plummeted, the man began selling a children's game he'd invented in order to keep his shop afloat. The game became an

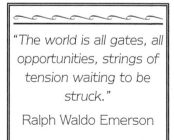

> *"The world is all gates, all opportunities, strings of tension waiting to be struck."*
>
> Ralph Waldo Emerson

overnight sensation. You've no doubt heard of *The Game of Life*. The man? Milton Bradley, one of the most successful publishers of board games in history, including such classics as *Operation, Chutes and Ladders, Candy Land* and *Twister.*

By the way, Lincoln also seemed to possess the surfer's knack for spotting rising opportunities. The decision to toss his razor was made after he received a letter from an eleven-year-old girl. She suggested that Lincoln would be more popular if he grew a beard! Can you imagine our sixteenth president without his famous beard? Why, he would seem positively unpresidential! And isn't that precisely the point?

Meanwhile, in Chicago, a busy professional woman is dumped by her fiancé. Eventually, she begins dating again. She's not into the bar scene, though, and tires quickly of being fixed up by friends and family members. When she consults a dating service, the experience is less than rewarding. Among other things, she feels stuck with her date for an entire evening even when she knows instantly there's no connection. She thinks, *Wouldn't it be nice if I could just meet someone for a brief time, say over lunch?*

> "Too many people are thinking of security instead of opportunity; they seem more afraid of life than of death."
>
> James F. Byrnes

Ten years later, *It's Just Lunch* is setting up quality lunch dates for busy professionals in all fifty states, as well as in England, France, Italy, Japan, Hong Kong, Singapore, Taiwan, Malaysia and Australia. Oh yeah, not only is the woman rich, she also found her soul mate in the process!

And herein lies a crucial difference between surfers and wannabes.

A surfer says, "Yes, and" to rising opportunities. "Yes, I see the wave, *and* I'm going for it." Wannabes, in contrast, say, "If only." "If only I could write." "If only I had more (time, money, whatever)." "If only I could do what I really like." "If only I could find someone to date or date someone *more* like that (smarter,

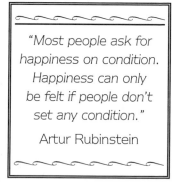

"*Most people ask for happiness on condition. Happiness can only be felt if people don't set any condition.*"

Artur Rubinstein

thinner, richer, prettier)." "If only (insert whatever crucial quality you feel your life is missing here), *then* I'd have the good life." As a result, wannabes rarely make it past the shoreline to where the waves are breaking. Once they do, the particular opportunity they'd spotted is often long gone.

Near the pristine waters of the archipelago off the west coast of Sweden lies a small village. Homes painted in solid colors of either red or yellow are spread out over the rocky landscape of the tightly knit community. Most families have lived in the area for generations. Actually, there's a long waiting list of people who'd like to live near the shore, but can't because environmental laws place strict limits on the number of houses that may be built in the area. And yet, one house stands curiously vacant and has done so for years.

"*I was seldom able to see an opportunity until it ceased to be one.*"

Mark Twain

The dwelling had once been home to a widow and her son. While in his youth, the widow's son met his one true love. Together, they planned a bright future, full of promise. Sadly, when the son approached his mother with the news, she forbade the union for fear of being left alone. Out of his loyalty and devotion, he acceded to her wish, and the wedding was called off.

Throughout the years, the lovers could only meet clandestinely. This continued until the time of the widow's death at age eighty-five. Believing they were finally able to realize their dream, the couple, now advanced in years themselves, quickly married. Within months, however, fate dealt the pair the cruelest of hands. The woman was struck with a fatal illness and died. The

> "Men do with opportunities as children do at the seashore; they fill their little hands with sand, and then let the grains fall through, one by one, till all are gone."
>
> T. Jones

man was left to finish his remaining years alone. When he died, the citizens of the small burg, moved by the tragedy, purchased the house to serve as a monument to both the power and folly of missed opportunities. It has stood empty ever since.

It's easy to feel sad about or wax nostalgic over missed opportunities. We say, "If I could go back and do it all over again, I'd . . ." or "If I knew then what I know now, I'd . . ." One of the funniest we ever heard was, "I wish I could live my life backwards." To this, surfers say: bogus. They know that the old saying "opportunity seldom knocks twice" is absolutely *true*. Why? Because, it's *always* knocking. In short, there are plenty more waves where those came from.

The constant beating of the waves is the cool thing about the surf. It's an endless summer of opportunities. Here's another way of looking at it: If you could spend one day at each place on the planet where people surf, you would not have to visit the same place twice for

decades.[2] So point your board toward the nearest horizon and *look for the waves that are on the rise now*. Of course, there's no guarantee that you'll catch one today. One thing is sure, however: If you're not out in the surf, you'll never ride.

Now, you may be thinking, *Nice idea guys, in theory. I'd like to believe that life is just a bowl of ~~cherries~~ (sorry) waves, too, and all I have to do to have the good life is reach out and touch one. But isn't this all really just a matter of dumb luck?*

The answer is, yes. Luck is involved in catching a wave. The surf is predictably *un*predictable. Spots that are normally hot can suddenly and unexpectedly iron out, becoming flat as a pancake. Waves that are breaking outside and to the right can change without warning , and start coming inside and to the left. Hey, the only place where waves are

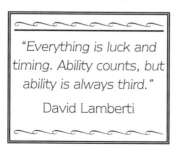

> "Everything is luck and timing. Ability counts, but ability is always third."
>
> David Lamberti

---

[2] *Endless Summer II*, New Line Studios, Bruce Brown, Director, 1994.

breaking the same way every day is in the wave pool at your local water park. And who hangs out there? We'll give you two guesses, and your first one doesn't count. Here's a hint: The answer is not surfers.

Let's face it, we humans place a high premium on predictability. To see just how much, all you have to do is take a drive across the country. In our towns and cities, variety has largely given

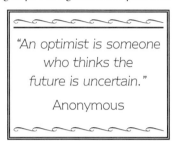

"An optimist is someone who thinks the future is uncertain."

Anonymous

way to uniformity. No matter where you go, it looks, tastes and *feels* the same as where you live. The same restaurants, same stores, same architecture, same basic attractions, etc.—the sign at the city limits of most places could now read, "You are entering Everywhere, U.S.A. Have a same day!" Isn't it strange? We complain about not having any luck, but we do everything we can to remove its influence from our lives.

For surfers, however, uncertainty is the whole point. It's what keeps them "frosty" and alert, on the lookout for incoming swells.

And because they can never know for sure where the next wave will come from or whether the wave they've spotted will be rideable or not, they set no preconditions for the experience. Tall or small, fast or slow, long or short, surfers ride them all. And therein lies the opportunity: riding whatever they can catch.

Take the issue of size, for example. Conventional wisdom says that for anything to be good, it's got to be big. Who in their right mind would say that less is more? After you've had a big-time *Fortune* 500 job or a big house in a prestigious neighborhood, who would be satisfied being a busboy living in a bungalow in the burbs?

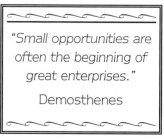

"Small opportunities are often the beginning of great enterprises."

Demosthenes

In surfing, however, there is no "minimum-wave law." Why? Because surfers know that the size of the swell and reward of the ride are not related. Something really stacked can suddenly and unexpectedly crumble on top and turn into a dribbler. Surfers are also familiar with "sleepers," waves that start out small, but end up packing a surprising zip.

Imagine how differently the story of William Wrigley might have ended had he let something as small and seemingly insignificant as chewing gum pass him by. Or consider the fall of the Berlin Wall in 1989. Over a forty-year period, politicians built their careers and Western governments spent literally billions of

"In great affairs, we ought to apply ourselves less to creating chances than to profiting from those that are offered."

François de La Rochefoucauld

dollars trying to topple this symbol of oppression and tyranny. And while its destruction is often attributed to such efforts, the truth is the whole rotten structure came tumbling down when people took advantage of an unexpected and seemingly inconsequential opportunity.

An official of the East German government was being interviewed on live television. The news conference was routine; the content ordinary. The man was spouting the same customary, tired, generic propaganda always heard on the state-run airwaves: Socialism was great, rah, rah, rah.

About midway through the meeting, a reporter asked the bureaucrat when the citizens of East Germany would be allowed to travel freely like people in the rest of Europe. In truth, because of deteriorating economic conditions within the small country, leaders of the Politburo had already decided on a plan. East Germans would be allowed to cross the border as long as they obtained a visa. Rather than stating the government position clearly, however, the official hastily replied, "They can go whenever they want, and nobody will stop them."

The statement took everyone by surprise. And though the official immediately tried to qualify his words, it was too late. The genie was out of the bottle. Within a few short hours, crowds gathered at the wall,

demanding that the border be opened. Guards, historically unwavering in their resolve, at first hesitated, but eventually relented to the wave of sentiment. The gates were opened. The East German government fell shortly thereafter. Within two short years, the events at the Wall had morphed into a tidal wave that swept away the entire Iron Curtain.

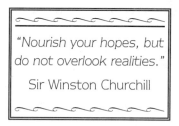

"Nourish your hopes, but do not overlook realities."

Sir Winston Churchill

Now, before running willy-nilly into the surf to catch that wave you just spotted, stop for a "heads-up"—a point of clarification, if you will. To some, it may sound like we're serving up some modern version of the old saying, "Eat drink and be merry for tomorrow you will die." That is, jump on any and all opportunities as they arise because you can never know when (or if) the next wave is coming.

So there is no misunderstanding, let us state clearly and for the record: Nothing could be further from the truth, or more foolhardy. Where wannabes rush in, surfers say, "Never enter the water without first knowing the bottom conditions."

Breaking off the north shore of Oahu, Hawaii, between the picturesque waters of Waimea Bay and the silky white sands of Sunset Beach, are the most famous waves in the world. They always have the starring role in any surfing flick and are a perennial favorite for the cover of glossy surfing monthlies. They are quintessential waves. Virtually everyone recognizes their iconic shape, even if they know little else about surfing. Towering waves curling into a perfectly formed hollow tube that seems to go on forever. The spot? The *Pipeline*.

Ask almost any surfer and they will tell you that riding "behind the curtain"—that is, inside the tube of a breaking wave—is the ultimate. It is, in fact, the highest scoring ride in surfing competitions—the most points being earned by those able to disappear into the tunnel and emerge before the wave collapses.

> "Good opportunities are
> not as important
> as favorable terrain."
>
> Mencius

Try catching one of the celebrated waves at the Pipeline without first checking out the bottom conditions, however, and you're much more likely to end up with a broken neck than a great ride. Why? Because, depending on where you are, the famous surf breaks on top of a coral reef resting a mere two inches to a couple of feet below the surface.

In life outside of surfing, empty bank accounts, relationships on the rocks and scuttled careers are but a few of the potentially nasty consequences awaiting those who jump on passing opportunities without first considering the bottom conditions. For example, when you're unhappy in your marriage, a coworker or colleague can start looking mighty attractive. Or if you're shy or socially awkward, a pint of Jack Daniels or the latest designer drug may make conviviality seem just one swallow away.

Few examples of this point could compete with the story of Bill Clinton. Whatever your politics, you've got to admire the "rags to riches" journey of the forty-second president of the United States. Indeed, his life is in many ways the living embodiment of the small town where he was born: Hope. This man who was reared in poverty and suffered abuse at the hands of his alcoholic stepfather went on to graduate from some of the world's most prestigious universities, was the youngest person ever to be elected governor of a state and, as president, presided over the longest peacetime expansion of the economy in the nation's history. Everyone knows what happened next. His brief affair with White House intern, Monica Lewinsky, erupted into a scandal that mired the remaining two years of his presidency in controversy.

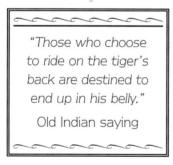

"Those who choose to ride on the tiger's back are destined to end up in his belly."

Old Indian saying

The sixty-four-thousand-dollar question is why anyone with so little to gain and so much to lose would ever take such a risk? Forget Clinton. What about Nixon, for gosh sakes? Talk about someone who ignored the bottom. Here's a man whose re-election to the presidency was in the bag. Yet, for whatever reason, he chose to put everything on the line without regard for the consequences.

We could cite numerous stories from life, history or literature that illustrate this point. In each instance, people used any number of rationalizations to justify venturing out into the surf without first checking out the bottom conditions. Here are a few:

- Opportunities like this come only once in a lifetime
- Everybody is doing it

• I've always managed before
• I deserve it
• No one has to know

Surfers know, however, that what you don't know can definitely hurt you. And since most beaches, like most aspects of life, come without warning signs or lifeguards, you've got to do your homework. You have to seriously consider the downside of any opportunity before hopping onboard. In this regard, one can only imagine how different the life paths of Bill Clinton or Richard Nixon would have been had they paused to reflect before acting.

This brings us right back to where we started. Which will you be? Surfer or wannabe? Of course, we can't tell what's going through your mind at this point. Maybe you're thinking that this whole "surfing thing" is a load of hooey and you wish you'd spent your money on something other than this book. (By the way, if this is the case, we'd appreciate your passing the book to the person sitting next to you on the plane, telling them in the process that it was so helpful

that you only needed to read two chapters to change your whole life.)

Another possibility is that you actually like the idea of surfing to the good life, but feel—at least right now—as if you don't have enough . . . whatever (time, money, equipment, etc.) to get on the board. Perhaps you're thinking, *Yes, this is a good idea . . . I'll do it . . . on the weekend, when the kids go to bed, when I've answered my last e-mail, on my two weeks of company-approved vacation time per year.* However, if this is what you're thinking, then you might just be a wannabe. At most, continuing to read the book will infringe on your already limited time. At worst, it'll be one of those good ideas you use to kick yourself in the pants rather than kick-start your life. Don't.

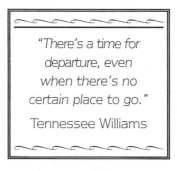

"There's a time for departure, even when there's no certain place to go."

Tennessee Williams

Maybe now is just not the time. So set the book down, spread your towel on the sand, slather on some sunscreen and enjoy.

A couple other outcomes can be imagined. You may be stoked, ready to "get high" on the next incoming wave. If this describes you, then you need read no further. You're ready for some helpful hints about the mechanics of surfing and *how* to catch a wave. Turn the page.

Another possibility is that you're still feeling uncertain, wondering, perhaps, if there are opportunities breaking in your life and, in the event there are, whether you'll be able to catch one. You're not alone if your feel this way. We certainly did. As mentioned in the last chapter, a number of opportunities were breaking in our lives. We'd even managed, as described in this chapter, to see these incoming swells. But we were hesitating, standing as it were, boards in hand at the shoreline of our lives. Could we do it, we wondered? Would we lose our just-*bearable* existences by pursuing something we could not know the outcome of in advance?

Ultimately, we ended up surfing. We did not boldly throw ourselves into the surf, however. Instead, our approach to getting our feet off solid ground might best be described as the "hokey-

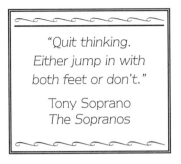

"Quit thinking. Either jump in with both feet or don't."

Tony Soprano
The Sopranos

pokey." We put one foot in, we took one foot out, we put the first one back in, and then we turned it all about. We started. We stopped. We inched forward and then pulled back. We went in further. We flirted with stopping altogether, and eventually we were surfing. As Surfmaster says, "Riding waves begins with putting one foot into the water. Left or right, it makes no difference."

If you are willing to take one step, turn the page.

3

From Wannabe to Surfer: How to Catch a Wave

Get a board,
Get to the beach,
A life of opportunities,
Is within your reach.

Anonymous

*A*ll right, dude! You did it! You've got one foot in the water. With a few more steps, you'll be out there with all the other surfers riding the waves, sitting on top of the world. We say, "Shaka, Shaka, brah!" (That's surfer lingo, by the way, for "right on!" If you could see us right now, we'd be giving you the hand signal that means the same thing—wiggling a raised hand with just the little finger and a thumb extended. All surfers do it. It's the not-so-secret handshake that conveys our shared experience: We know what the good life is all about.)

Whatever you're feeling at this point, now is not the time to look around for support from the people frolicking in the sea foam or lying around on the beach. Not wanting to be reminded of their own just-bearable existences, they're more likely to discourage than encourage you. "Hey, come back," you might hear them calling as you venture out into the surf. "There's a great volleyball game about to start." Or maybe they'll just shout warnings in your general direction, "Hey, are you nuts?! You can get killed out there. Stay with us."

Your fellow surfers may not be all that supportive either. Anxious to get in as many rides as possible before the beach (and the water) fills up with tourists, they're likely to shun any shoreline chitchat. You might even end up on the receiving end of a bit of hazing. "Hey hodad, you left your plastic bucket and shovel on the beach." Or, "Where'd *you* learn to surf, kid? Nebraska?"

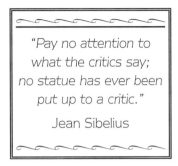

> "Pay no attention to what the critics say; no statue has ever been put up to a critic."
>
> Jean Sibelius

We say, "Ignore all this and keep your eyes on the prize." Remember, you're here to surf. Set after set of bodacious waves are breaking right now just a few feet from where you're standing. All you have to do to catch one is follow three basic steps:

- Paddle out
- Position
- Pop up

Here's the skinny on each.

Step One: Paddling Out

Mose Gastin, a young child with a big dream, wanted to be in show business—a star of stage and screen. From around the age of two, he traveled across the country performing with his father as part of the Will Mastin Trio. "We rarely remained in one place more than a week," the wee-wannabe later wrote of his experience. "Packing suitcases and riding on trains and buses were as natural to me as a stroll in a carriage might be to another child."

The group worked tremendously hard at perfecting its act, always innovating and updating, continually tweaking their performance to give audiences the best entertainment possible. Many sacrifices were made in pursuit of their objective—family ties and an education were but two. And yet, as hard as Mose and the others worked, fame and fortune always seemed to elude the trio.

It's not as though the troupe never, to borrow a phrase from show business, "got an even break." Along the way, several famous entertainers extended a helping hand. Dancer Bill "Bojangles" Robinson, big band leaders Tommy Dorsey and Count Basie, crooner Frank Sinatra, television variety-show host Eddie Cantor, and movie stars Ava Gardner and Mickey Rooney were just a few of the headliners to give the struggling act a shot at stardom. Neither could one say that the group was actually *un*successful. Audiences always seemed to appreciate the trio, calling the performers out for at least one encore on most occasions. At the end of the day, however, rather than living the glamorous and exalted life of the Hollywood elite, the group shuffled from one fleabag hotel to another, often going to bed hungry.

And then it happened. Years of huffing it across the stages of America put the group at *the right place at the right time.* "The classic fallacy of show business," the entertainer observed many years later, "is, 'Someday you'll get your break, and then it'll be all velvet for you.' It's a lovely dream, but untrue."

What, in his opinion, made the difference? The trio simply persisted, evolving and adapting, passionately pursuing their dream until "the combination of circumstances was finally right and it all fell in place, like when the three cherries on a slot machine all come up at once." While his family called him Mose, you know this person as Sammy Davis, Jr. [3,4]

[3] Davis, Sammy, Jr. et al. *Sammy: An Autobiography.* New York: Farrar, Straus & Giroux, 2000, pp. 109–110.

[4] Davis, p. 14.

Surfers know all too well about persistence in the pursuit of waves. They say: If you want to surf, you'd better be prepared to paddle—from the shoreline out to where the waves are breaking, then forward and back across the surf in pursuit of the next incoming set, and finally, once in position, grabbing handfuls of water in an attempt to seize the rising opportunity. "The true nuts and bolts of surfing," observes surfer Hope Winsworth, "is paddling."

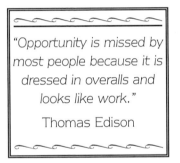

"Opportunity is missed by most people because it is dressed in overalls and looks like work."

Thomas Edison

If this sounds like *work* to you, we say, think again. Surfers *do* expend a tremendous amount of energy, but few would describe it as work. Rather, they'd say they're "stoked"—stirred to action by an inner flame, a passion that may leave them feeling "noodle-armed" at the end of the day, but also alive and full of joy.

So what is work? That's when your efforts feel more like treading water than making progress; it's when thrashing about leaves you afloat but not fulfilled. Over time, you end up exhausted, feeling like you're slowly drowning—becoming physically, mentally and spiritually kaput.

With that said, we must admit there are people who seem to get all the breaks. They're born super-gifted or talented, appear to have inherited a permanent "get-a-good-life-for-free" card, or are just plain lucky. It's as though this privileged group of winners doesn't have to go in search of the proverbial pot of gold at the end of the rainbow. It magically materializes in their laps. In surfing lingo, the waves come to them rather than them having to paddle out to the waves. In our experience, however, this is extremely rare—romantic,

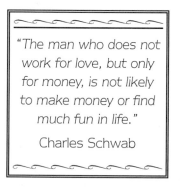

"The man who does not work for love, but only for money, is not likely to make money or find much fun in life."

Charles Schwab

yes, but largely the stuff of Hollywood fantasies.

What's more, in surfing there's really only one set of circumstances under which waves are likely to come to you: a hurricane! Much more common, surfers point their boards out to sea, paddle out to where the waves are breaking and then work feverishly to place themselves in the path of rising opportunity. Even then, there are no guarantees.

Returning to the frustrating and fantastic voyage of Sammy Davis Jr., we pointed out earlier how he struggled for many years, continuing to work as a support act rather than a headliner, despite receiving help from many of the biggest stars of his day. When Ed Sullivan called to book the trio on his television program, Davis thought the group been given the "big break" they needed. In the 1950s and '60s, Sullivan's prime-time Sunday evening variety show was *the* way new talent was introduced to the entertainment-hungry American public. Remember Elvis? How about Bob Hope, Lena Horne, Dean Martin, Jerry Lewis, Albert Schweitzer, Irving Berlin, Fred Astaire or the Beatles? All made their television debut on that influential program.

Believing that their paddling had put them in the right place at the right time, Davis and the group gave a picture-perfect performance. They sang and danced like never before. Sammy did his best impressions. There was only one glitch: No picture was broadcast. Literally. For the first time in television history, the coaxial cable that carried the program had broken, blacking out every television screen in America!

At that point, few would have faulted the trio had they thrown up their hands in despair and quit the business altogether. Entertainment was their passion, however, and so the performers quickly paddled back into the fray, scanning the horizon and working to place themselves in the path of the next set of waves. And it didn't take long to arrive. In the weeks following the program, sympathetic stories about the mishap, along with pictures of Davis and his group, appeared in newspapers across the country. "It drew more attention and caused more talk about us," he later recalled, "than if everything had gone smoothly." Within a very short time, their persistence transformed a crumbling wave into the ride of their professional lives.

Surfmaster says: Beware of flatlanders promising the "no-paddle take-off." As the name implies, this involves catching a wave *without* first having to paddle the board. While experienced surfers would acknowledge that the maneuver is possible, they'd also warn you not to hold your breath as it is exceedingly rare. Virtually every scam, whether solicited through the mail or promoted on television, makes a similar claim. Take this pill and lose weight (or live longer). Wear this fragrance and drive the opposite sex crazy. Make money without having to leave your home. Pay the psychic and know your future. In short, no paddling required. Right!

Ever heard of Cyrus Field? It's not like he's a household name or something. Truth is, though, the work and passion of this then-thirty-three-year-old entrepreneur affects the lives of most Americans on a daily basis. The year was 1854. And while it may be difficult to imagine given the near instantaneous communication our world presently enjoys, sending a message from North America to Europe took upwards of two months.

A mere decade earlier, the telegraph had burst on the scene. The invention spread like wildfire across the United States. Cables were hung on poles connecting what had once been separated by thousands of miles and countless perils. In the process, the way Americans thought, worked and lived was forever changed.

Cyrus Field dreamed of changing the relationship between America and Europe in precisely the same way: by a cable.[5] In this case, a three-thousand-mile long cable spread along the ocean bottom

[5] Gordon S. J. A. *Thread Across the Ocean: The Heroic Story of the Transatlantic Cable.* New York: Walker & Company, 2002.

from Newfoundland to Ireland. Field's contemporaries thought he was nuts. The ocean was vast and unforgiving. And everyone knew that travel between the two continents was dangerous and slow.

For twelve long years he paddled against a tide of negative sentiment. Gradually, a wave of interest in the project began building. By 1857, everything was in place. The project appeared to be doomed from the start, however. Immediately after setting out from Ireland, the machinery used to lay the cable failed. Even worse, the gauge of wire chosen proved too small and flimsy to withstand the harsh Atlantic environment. Four hundred miles were lost at sea. Cyrus Field was mocked and heckled.

One year later, he was back at it with a stronger cable and even greater resolve. Rather than using one boat to drop a single cable all the way from Ireland to Newfoundland, this time he decided to use two boats, each starting in the middle and setting out in opposite directions. The plan worked! Queen Victoria sent a ninety-nine-word message to President James Buchanan. A huge celebration followed. The party was short-lived, however. Over the next three weeks, the signals coming through the cable began to weaken and then died completely.

Twice Field had set out and now twice he'd failed—miserably and

CYRUS FIELD KEPT PADDLING UNTIL HE CONNECTED TWO CONTINENTS!

THAT'S AN IDEA WORTH CONNECTING WITH!

publicly. At this point, most people would have given up and abandoned ship. For his part, Field took what he learned from each attempt and went back to work. He was a surfer extraordinaire. He knew and lived the first step of catching a wave: Keep paddling. It would take him two more tries and eight additional years to connect the two continents successfully.

Historians note that Field's innovation and accomplishment set the stage for the establishment of the United States as a world power. And there's more: Overnight, the world had become a much smaller place. The transatlantic connection initiated a major shift in the collective psychology of humanity that continues today with the Internet and World Wide Web.

Paddling pays!

Step Two: Positioning

Let's stop and review. You've made your way to the beach. Eyes raised, you've looked beyond the mass of humanity clustered along the shoreline of life and noticed the incoming waves. If you can't actually see those bodacious opportunities from where you're standing—a fog, fellow tourists on the beach, something obscures your view—you can at least hear or feel them breaking. Endlessly and without effort, they rise and fall, roll in and out, beckoning—a reminder of the

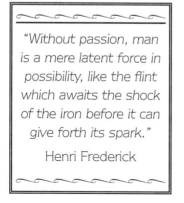

"Without passion, man is a mere latent force in possibility, like the flint which awaits the shock of the iron before it can give forth its spark."

Henri Frederick

many possibilities lying just within your reach.

However you've lived your life until now, whatever hesitancy you might experience at this moment, you wade in, mindful that the good life lies before, *not* behind you. You'll want to keep this awareness close to your heart because fear, fatigue and the sheer force of the breaking waves will soon be fighting you, opposing your progress, even pushing you back to the beach.

With a surfer's determination, you inch forward, taking first one step and then another. Finally, when the water is about waist high, you set your board down and lay on top of it. Then you start paddling. Then some more. And then more. And you keep paddling until you reach the "line-up," that point where the waves are consistently *starting* to break. You've made it. You're in the neighborhood—the surf zone.

Once here, most surfers push themselves up, straddle the board and take a breather. However, while doing so, they keep their eyes trained on the water, scanning the surf for any telltale signs of incoming swells: ripples, bulges, white caps, the movement of other surfers, anything that says, "This looks promising." It doesn't matter who spots the wave first. The key at this point is "positioning"—maneuvering your board to the spot where the force and power of the wave can catch and move you along.

> "It is a secret which every intellectual man quickly learns, that beyond the energy of his possessed and conscious intellect he is capable of a new energy . . . by the abandonment to the nature of things . . . he can draw . . . the ethereal tides to roll and circulate through him."
>
> Ralph Waldo Emerson

Now before you move on, take a moment and revisit that last sentence. Positioning is all about putting yourself in the spot where the wave can *catch you*. And finding the "heart" of any given wave is part art, part skill and, frankly, part luck. The ocean, like life itself, is dynamic, always in motion and constantly changing. For this reason, there's no simple formula, no guidebook, no GPS device that can reliably point the way.

With that said, two facts are certain. Positioned too far out in front of a wave and "over the falls" you'll go, first hurled to the bottom and then sucked back up the face to be launched again. On the other hand, if you're positioned too far behind, the wave will simply pass you by. Stick with it, though, and over time you'll develop "surf-sense," a feeling for the pulse of a wave—its direction, movement and power. There are still no guarantees. You won't catch every one, *but more will catch you* (more on this later).

In the meantime, consider the story of Carolyn Naselii, one person who literally positioned herself in the "heart" of a breaking wave. For twenty years, she worked as an attorney, first dealing with brokenhearted couples in divorce proceedings and then later serving as a judicial hearing officer in juvenile court.

Perhaps because of her work, Carolyn loved hearts. They were her hobby. She collected them, decorated her house with them. She even dreamed of one day opening her own store featuring exclusively—you guessed it—hearts. Clothing, plates, bowls, artwork, rings, purses, linens, photographs—anything—items for women, men, children or adults, as long as the piece was in the shape of or in some way featured a heart.

For years, Carolyn toyed with the idea. "Then one day," she later recalled, "I said, 'I'm going to do it.'" And she did. First she did her homework, though, scanning the horizon from the safety of the shoreline to see whether opportunities were on the rise for such a store. Finding that the market for hearts was barely tapped, she made her way down to the water and began wading out.

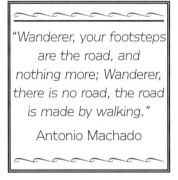

"Wanderer, your footsteps are the road, and nothing more; Wanderer, there is no road, the road is made by walking."

Antonio Machado

With the help of her daughter, she found the perfect location for the shop, a warm and welcoming storefront on a tree-lined street in the heart of one of Chicago's most established and desired areas. The presence of other thriving businesses, fashionable eateries and trendy boutiques was a strong clue that she was in the right neighborhood—in surfing lingo, the "line up" or surf zone.

Heartbeats has now been in business for several years. The shop and Carolyn have been featured in a number of newspaper and magazine articles, including *Skyline* and *Chicago Woman*. For her part, Carolyn is quick to note that it's not always been smooth sailing. Along the way, there have been considerable challenges. For example, seven months after opening, her thirty-nine-year-old daughter was killed in a car accident, leaving her to raise her two grandchildren. Still, she maintains, "I have no regrets." During the tough times, her passion sustained her, kept her going. If you peek in the windows of her shop on a Saturday afternoon, you might even catch a glimpse of Carolyn with her grandkids. It seems that hearts run in the family.

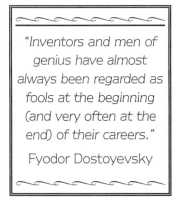

"Inventors and men of genius have almost always been regarded as fools at the beginning (and very often at the end) of their careers."

Fyodor Dostoyevsky

Now, contrast this last account with the tale of Ignaz Semmelweis, a Hungarian-born physician who worked in Vienna, Austria, during the mid-1800s. The good doctor was alarmed by the number of women who died in hospitals following childbirth—as many as 30 percent (that's nearly one in three women) in some locations. Physicians at the time attributed the high mortality rates to "bad air" or "bedside fever," the latter a condition believed to result from women's feelings of guilt and remorse around the issues of sex and childbirth.

Such explanations made little sense to Dr. Semmelweis. After all, he'd noticed that women attended by midwives—in spite of breathing the same air and having the same supposed "issues"—were much less likely to develop the diseases or die. He started to investigate, looking for an explanation by comparing and contrasting the activities and practices of physicians and midwives. It didn't take him long to notice one important difference: Physicians, unlike midwives, frequently came into contact with multiple patients and even corpses during their daily hospital routine. Suspecting that the doctors might be spreading the disease themselves, he suggested hand washing between patients. The results were immediate and dramatic. In those settings where strict hand washing was observed, the death rate dropped to 1 percent!

Nowadays, nearly everyone knows how germs are spread. We're reminded daily by signs posted in restrooms, lectures in school, as well as a steady diet of images on television melodramas showing physicians vigorously scrubbing their hands before surgery. As obvious as this may seem to us now, however, it was not common knowledge during the mid-1800s. *Semmelweis was ahead of his time.* And while later generations would benefit from his observations and discovery, he personally suffered the consequences of anyone positioned in front of a breaking wave. He was ridiculed and his theory rejected. Depressed over the deaths caused by failure to adopt simple sanitation procedures, Semmelweis eventually ended up in a sanitarium. In an ironic and tragic twist of fate, he died after a cut on his finger became infected.

MANY GREAT INNOVATERS HAVE BEEN WRITTEN OFF AS MAD!

THEN CONGRATULATIONS— YOU MAY WELL BE THE GREATEST ONE THIS CENTURY'S EVER SEEN!

You don't have to think very hard to conjure up a list of people who were positioned ahead of the wave and suffered as a result:

- Hypatia . . . fourth-century *female* mathematician, astronomer and philosopher . . . seized on the street, beaten, dragged to a church, flayed with sharp tiles and then burned to death.
- Galileo Galilei . . . proved that the sun was at the center of the solar system . . . excommunicated from his church and placed on house arrest for the rest of his life . . . spared execution only because he agreed to write a book and declare publicly that he was wrong!
- The Pilgrims . . . after surviving the hazardous waters of the Atlantic, nearly half of the 102 men, women and children who left England in search of religious freedom on the American continent died during the first winter.
- Vincent van Gogh . . . introduced bright colors and a novel style that eventually spawned the expressionist movement . . . widely believed to be the most well-known and recognizable artist in history . . . he sold only one painting during his lifetime . . . in and out of asylums . . . died from a self-inflicted gunshot to the head.
- Madame Curie . . . twentieth-century scientist who discovered radium . . . pioneered the first x-ray machine for use in medicine . . . won two Nobel prizes . . . went blind and eventually died from exposure to radiation.
- Martin Luther King . . . civil-rights leader . . . advocated peaceful protest and nonviolent direct action . . . sparked the conscience of a generation . . . at thirty-five years of age, the youngest man ever awarded the Nobel Peace prize . . . cut down by an assassin's bullet at age thirty-nine.

As these stories indicate, an element of tragedy often surrounds those later recognized as ahead of their time. Yes, they are honored and their memory revered, but more often in death than in life. And while those who come later benefit greatly from their efforts, the visionaries themselves frequently find their own "good life" cut short—if they experience it at all. Surfmaster says: Such are the risks of being positioned in front of a wave. The breaks can be hard and unforgiving.

Don't get us wrong. We're not dissing innovation, ambition or character—standing up for what you believe. What we *are* saying is that innovation and ambition are meaningless in the absence of a wave to carry them along. Surfers know: no waves, no ride. To experience the good life, passion must intersect with opportunity.

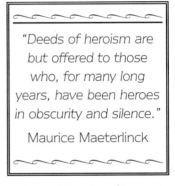

"Deeds of heroism are but offered to those who, for many long years, have been heroes in obscurity and silence."

Maurice Maeterlinck

So if that's what happens when you're positioned too far out in front of a wave, what about being too far behind? Ever heard of Walter Bimson? Unless you're a collector of architectural arcana, his name is probably unknown to you. In 1947, however, Mr. Bimson had a shot at the good life. He was in the right place at the right time.

As the story goes, Bimson commissioned avant-garde architect Frank Lloyd Wright to draw up plans for a bank that was to be located in Phoenix, Arizona. Given Wright's philosophy of integrating buildings into the surrounding landscape and topography, he designed a structure with an open roof. *The Daylight Bank*, as he named it, would capitalize on the abundant desert sunlight. Additionally, hoping to reflect the easy-going lifestyle of the local inhabitants, Wright added an element to the plans that had never been thought of before: a drive-up window.

Bimson and the board of directors would have nothing of it. They rejected the plans out of hand. A drive-up window? For them, that was just . . . well . . . too much. No one would ever use it! Banking was just too *personal*. People would always want to have face-to-face contact with the person handling their money.

As the old saying goes, "Famous last words." While the structure was never built, drive-up windows, ATMs and Internet banking are, as everyone knows, the wave of the present. Who knows how Bimson and his banking buddies might be remembered today—*how good their lives might have been*—had they gotten onboard in 1947! As it stands, the only chance that someone will encounter their names today is if they tour Talisien West—the winter residence of Frank Lloyd Wright located in Scottsdale, Arizona—and happen across the paper model of the structure that sits alone on a table in one of the many rooms of the house. If you happen to visit, ask your guide to tell you the story.

People discovered in retrospect to have been seriously *behind* the times—that is, to have been in the right place at the right time and yet missed a breaking opportunity—are remembered with a feeling of mild amusement (if they are remembered at all). The upside of being positioned *behind* a breaking wave, however, is that it is safer. Let's face it, no surfer ever drowned, suffered great bodily injury or died from missing a wave. Sure, your ego might take a bruising from the heckling you'll receive now and then from other surfers. You might even feel a tad bit lonely as you watch your buds being swept up and moved along by the waves you let pass. All in all, however, the biggest risk you face is ending up with a terrible case of the "if onlys."

Unless you know a great deal about the history of rock and roll, you've probably never heard of Tony Meechan or Dick Rowe. During the 1960s, both worked for Decca Records. Tony was a drummer who'd made it big as the acquisition and recording (A&R) man for the label. Dick was the head of the company.

On New Year's Eve 1961, a young group of wannabe musicians entered Decca Studios. By the way, it was no small feat getting an audition for the struggling act. Just like nowadays, there were lots of bands and each and every one dreamed of hitting it big. The only reason this unknown group pulled it off was because their manager knew someone, who knew someone else, who was in a position to arrange the whole thing.

Needless to say, the group was stoked. They set up and started playing. Within two hours, they'd recorded around twenty tunes, and the audition came to an end. "That was it," one of the band members later recalled. "We left and went back to our hotel." And they waited. And waited. And then waited some more.

Full of anticipation and hope, the manager of the group eventually started contacting the company to find out whether the group would be signed. All Tony Meechan would say, however, was, "I'm a busy man." Then he'd give the manager the brush-off. In true Hollywood style, he'd say something like, "Yeah, baby . . . let's do lunch . . . soon."

Eventually, the group did hear from the company, and the news was not good. "Guitar groups are on the way out," Decca executive Dick Rowe explained to the band's manager. And then the company immediately signed Brian Poole and the Tremeloes instead! Dick Rowe and Tony Meecham have probably been kicking themselves ever since as they let the biggest wave in rock and roll history pass them by: The Beatles.[6] Can you say, "If only . . . "?

---

[6] McCartney, Paul, et al. *The Beatles Anthology.* San Francisco, Calif.: Chronicle Books, 2000, p. 67.

While stories of the big one that got away are somewhat harder to find, they do exist:

- Recall the story about the fall of the Berlin Wall in the previous chapter? Consider this: Just a few short years before this momentous event, foreign-affairs correspondent Flora Lewis (ever heard of her?) boldly asserted, "Any realistic sense of the world today leaves it clear that there isn't going to be any German reunification this century, *nor probably in the lifetime of anyone who can read this.*" For our part, we're glad the Germans didn't listen to Flora.

- Or how about an entry in the diary of King George III of England on July 4, 1776. It reads, "Nothing of importance happened on this day." Go figure.

- Then there's Irving Fisher. Six weeks before the catastrophic drop in stock prices that plunged the United States into the Great Depression, this economist confidently asserted, "There may be a recession in stock prices, but not anything in the nature of a crash." (Not that economic prognosticators are any better at predicting trends in the current market, eh?)

- In 1945, a now defunct publishing house wrote the author George Orwell explaining their reason for rejecting the manuscript of his book, *Animal Farm*. "It is impossible to sell animal stories in the U.S.A." Uh-huh. Tell that to the millions of high-school and college students who read the classic as part of their English literature courses!

- Finally, consider the director of the Blue Book Modeling Agency, Emmeline Snively, who advised an attractive yet awkward, wannabe movie star to "learn secretarial work or else get married." While Snively is long forgotten, the average person knows this young woman by her professional and given name: Norma Jean Mortensen (also known as Marilyn Monroe).

We could go on and on, from Heinrich Rudolf Hertz—the person who discovered radio waves and whose name is unknowingly used by people to this day when referring to the location of their favorite station on the radio dial (as in, kilo-*Hertz* [kHz], mega-*Hertz* [mHz])—who declared that the "waves I have discovered will [not] have any practical application" to physicist Lee De Forest who asserted that, "Man will never reach the moon, regardless of all future scientific advances"—the latter making his prediction just twelve short years before the first successful landing on the moon. Anyway, you get the idea. And the list is endless.

So what's a surfer to do? Well, first cut yourself a little slack. While no one purposefully tries to be in front of a breaking wave, even the best surfers get crunched every now and then. Most start-up businesses fail

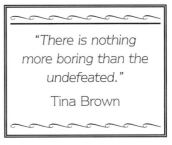

"*There is nothing more boring than the undefeated.*"

Tina Brown

within the first year, for example. Would you believe that in the past century alone there have been three hundred automobile manufacturers?

Missing the occasional wave is also a part of surfing. Sure, it's frustrating, especially when everyone but you seemed to see it coming (and had the ride of their lives as a result). But it's going to happen. So relax.

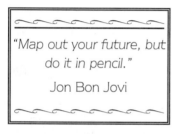

"Map out your future, but do it in pencil."

Jon Bon Jovi

Second? Stay flexible. As strange as it may sound, people who find themselves on a steady diet of sand and coral as a result of always being out in front of breaking waves suffer from the exact same problem as those who seem to miss every opportunity that comes their way. They've got an idea—a vision, a plan or a scheme—about the way things *should* be, and they cling to it for dear life. The first one says, "It's gotta be this wave," and then paddles like crazy. The other is always saying, "Eh, it's not this wave. I'll wait till the next one (or the next one or the next one)." As a result, both are chronically out of sync—constantly one stroke ahead or behind—with rising opportunities.

Think of it this way: Opportunities, like the surf, are always rolling in—many more than any one surfer can possibly ride to success. For this reason, there's no need to force it, to make the ride happen. After all, *there will always be another wave.* At the same time, you can't expect the

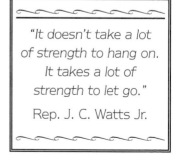

"It doesn't take a lot of strength to hang on. It takes a lot of strength to let go."

Rep. J. C. Watts Jr.

READER/CUSTOMER CARE SURVEY

We care about your opinions. Please take a moment to fill out this Reader Survey card and mail it back to us. As a special **"thank you"** we'll send you exciting news about interesting books and a valuable **Gift Certificate.**

Please PRINT using ALL CAPS

First Name _____ MI. ____ Last Name _____

Address _____

ST ____ Zip _____ Email: _____ City _____

Phone # (___) _____ Fax # (___) _____ Comments:

(1) Gender:

_____ Female _____ Male

(2) Age:

_____ 12 or under _____ 40-59
_____ 13-19 _____ 60+
_____ 20-39

(3) What attracts you most to a book?
(Please rank 1-4 in order of preference.)

	1	2	3	4
3) Title	○	○	○	○
4) Cover Design	○	○	○	○
5) Author	○	○	○	○
6) Content	○	○	○	○

(7) Where do you usually buy books?
*Please fill in your top **TWO** choices.*

1) _____ Bookstore
2) _____ Religious Bookstore
3) _____ Online
4) _____ Book Club/Mail Order
5) _____ Price Club (Costco, Sam's Club, etc.)
6) _____ Retail Store (Target, Wal-Mart, etc.)

BB4

BUSINESS REPLY MAIL

FIRST-CLASS MAIL   PERMIT NO 45   DEERFIELD BEACH, FL

POSTAGE WILL BE PAID BY ADDRESSEE

HEALTH COMMUNICATIONS, INC.
3201 SW 15TH STREET
DEERFIELD BEACH FL 33442-9875

ocean to dish up a wave that suits you. It's not your personal pond. And like the world in general, it obeys forces that are completely outside of your control. Stay flexible, however, and you'll increase the chances of positioning yourself for success—that spot where passing opportunities can catch and carry you along.

Step Three: Popping Up

If positioning is all about maintaining one's flexibility, then "popping up" is, in a word, all about *commitment*—literally choosing to *take a stand*. At this point, you've already done all the hard work. You paddled out (and often around and around). You dealt with the elements (e.g., the cold water, choppy surf and perhaps chilly send-off of those at the shoreline of your life). Somehow you've managed to stay afloat en route (no small feat when you're cold and tired). You even managed to position yourself in the path of an incoming wave that has caught and is now moving you along.

YOU'VE GOT
TO POP UP...
TO STOP YOUR
DREAMS GOING
≥ POP ≤ !

To complete the process—to take it to the next level—*to be a surfer,* you must move from a prone to a standing position. Simply put, you have to commit: It's going to be this wave, at this moment, no matter what has come before or may follow after. And then, without hesitation or further deliberation—*and in one deft move*—you have to act. You must stand up.

Popping up is key to experiencing the fullness and richness of the opportunities a wave can provide. It allows the surfer to harness the power of the wave, to have influence, to bend, tweak and finesse, to be a partner rather than a pawn in how events unfold.

Sure, it's possible to ride with your body laying flat on the board. In fact, some people never move from the horizontal to the vertical position. But that ain't surfing. Indeed, surfers use a variety of expressions when referring to such folk, including belly-rider, flatman, foam flapper, tea bag, toilet lid and doormat. As you can surmise from the tone, in the surfer's mind, such riding is a half-measure—a pale comparison to the real deal.

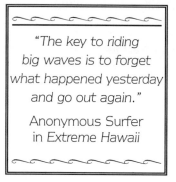

"The key to riding big waves is to forget what happened yesterday and go out again."

Anonymous Surfer
in *Extreme Hawaii*

As negatively as surfers describe belly-riding, in the modern world it's easy to understand why people end up traveling through life flat on their stomachs. Indeed, many of us, if asked, would say we have little choice in the matter. The pace and seeming complexity of life leaves us feeling pressed to whatever supports or buoys us up—however unfulfilling that might ultimately be. We can't stand up and take full advantage of the opportunities presented to us because we are, in effect, forced to hang on for dear life.

Take technology, for example. You can't turn on the television, leaf through a magazine or connect to the Internet without being bombarded with calls to upgrade, retool or jump on the latest innovation bandwagon. The good life, we are told, is the next purchase away—the newest software, the latest edition of Windows™, the sleekest cell phone, the fastest CPU, the flattest computer monitor (or television screen), and most recently, the smallest device containing as many of the above features as possible.

Of course, there is nothing inherently wrong with being on the cutting edge of technology. We're no neo-Luddites, viewing the past through rose-colored glasses and advocating a return to the simplicity of the pre-information age. The problem is

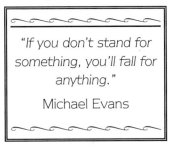

"If you don't stand for something, you'll fall for anything."

Michael Evans

that few of us ever use anything beyond even the most basic functions of the last technologic wonder we acquired before we've been seduced into buying the next generation.

For example, in spite of their many capabilities, the computer remains for most people a glorified typewriter, the cell phone merely a phone you can use outdoors. Windows™ is still a window to frustration, the Internet a twenty-four-hour portal for pop-up ads and unsolicited e-mail, and PDAs are basically back-lighted, battery-powered schedule and address books. Get this:

"The knowledge that something remains yet unenjoyed impairs our enjoyment of the good before us."

Samuel Johnson

Astronauts flew to the moon on less computing power than exists in most home PCs. And yet many of us still haven't figured out how to program our VCR, for heaven's sake. Don't worry about that, though, as it's time to chuck that old technology anyway and upgrade to DVD!

The point is that when faced with a never ending succession of possibilities, committing to any one ends up feeling like a luxury we can ill afford. Once something new comes along, promising to be better, faster or more advanced, no one wants to risk missing out, being left behind or falling off the razor's edge. In reality, however, by constantly grasping at what might lie ahead, we lose out on the fullness and richness of the opportunities already within our grasp.

Nowhere is this pattern of looking to the next wave rather than committing to the present one more poignant than in our intimate relationships, ultimately robbing us of the good life. As an example, consider the movie adaptation of Nick Hornby's internationally bestselling novel, *High Fidelity.* If you haven't seen the flick, but find yourself—in spite of your tireless efforts to locate that special someone—always coming up short in the relationship department, then get to your nearest video store and rent it as soon as possible.

In the film, actor John Cusack plays lead character Rob Gordon. He is the owner of a semi-failing record store and a man with a long history of wrecked relationships. Sure, he's had scads, some of them even quite intense. But something is always missing: that special, unidentifiable, intangible quality that makes one want to commit, that allows a person to happily forgo any and all possible future relationships and say with certainty, "Yes! *This* is the one."

Anyway, as the movie (and the book) opens, Gordon's latest live-in girlfriend, Laura, played by Danish actress Iben Hjejle, is moving out of the apartment they've shared for the last several years. Gordon is surprised and dumbstruck by Laura's decision to end their relationship. After she leaves, he berates himself in private, "What's wrong with me?" he asks and then continues, "Seriously. What happened? Why am I doomed to be left? Doomed to be rejected? I need answers."

In between his half-hearted management of his record store and meager (but hopeful) attempts to win back Laura's affection, Gordon searches for an answer. First, he rationalizes. "Nowadays, with the fast pace of the world and all, maybe relationships simply aren't meant to last." And while this thought is temporarily soothing, it is ultimately unsatisfying, implying as it does, a future filled with more of the same.

Next, he starts contacting all of his former girlfriends, beginning with his first romance, Alison Ashworth in the sixth grade. That relationship, he recalls with surprise, ended as abruptly as it had started. They were an item before recess. By

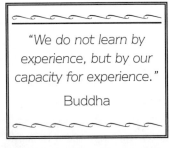

"We do not learn by experience, but by our capacity for experience."

Buddha

afternoon, she had left him for another boy. Though years have passed, he still can't figure out what happened. And while, he says, "It would be nice to think that times have changed . . . relationships have become more sophisticated, skins thicker, instincts more developed," he recognizes that, "All of my romantic stories are a scrambled version of that first one." In the end, he is forced to conclude that the answer he seeks will not be found by sifting through the ashes of his personal history.

Right around this time, Gordon learns that Laura is seeing someone new. Knowing there is a realistic chance she may be gone for good, he becomes a man on a mission. Whether he chooses ultimately to stay with Laura or not is unimportant. His job at the moment is to win her back!

He pulls out all the stops. He calls, sends flowers, asks her on dates, begs her to concede there is a chance, however small, that the two of them might get back together. And as soon as she says, "Yes, about a 9 percent chance," Gordon promptly runs off and sleeps with a woman he met recently at a bar. It's a strange and unhappy pattern he's noticed before. "If I can convince myself that Laura does want me a bit," he observes, "then I'll be okay again . . . I can cope without her, because then I won't want her, and I can get on with looking for someone else."[7]

He puzzles over the seeming paradox in his behavior: He doesn't want what he has until he doesn't have it and always wants what he doesn't have until he does. Exasperated, he shouts out, "When's it all going to stop?" He knows his life is bankrupt. And he's tired. "Tired," he says, "of the fantasy." Why? "'Cause it really doesn't exist . . . and there never really are any surprises . . . *and it really never delivers.*"

And then it strikes him—the answer he was seeking all along. "I never really *committed* to Laura," he realizes. "I always had one foot out the door, and *that* prevented me from doing a lot of things . . . like thinking about my future. I guess it made more sense to commit to nothing, keep my options open . . . and that's *suicide,* by tiny . . . tiny . . . increments."

Wait. Wait. Hold that thought for a moment. . . .

Surfmaster paddles out to the line-up, sits up and straddles his

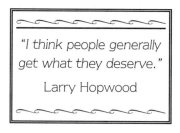

"I think people generally get what they deserve."

Larry Hopwood

---

[7] Hornby, N. *High Fidelity.* Great Britain: Indigo, 1995, p. 94.

board. "The waves were so much better the day before," says a guy floating nearby. "You should have seen 'em," he adds, and begins recounting with excitement some of yesterday's rides. "I hear a storm front is approaching," another chimes in, "so the waves are bound to be better tomorrow."

Turning to face Surfmaster, the first then asks, "What do you think?" Without missing a stroke, Surfmaster says, "Watch this," and in one deft move pops up and catches the wave before them. As he is carried out of sight, the two hear him say, "Every wave I catch is the best wave of my life."

> "To heal psychic ailments that we have contracted through misfortunes or faults of our own, understanding avails nothing, reasoning little, time much, but resolute action everything."
>
> Johann Wolfgang von Goethe

That's not to say that surfers don't ever dream of better waves. They do—*but not when they're already surfing.* Ever watch a surfing movie? You know, flicks with names like *Endless Summer* or *Extreme Hawaii?* As longtime observer of the scene, Thad Ziolkowski, points out in his memoir *On a Wave,* films in this genre are nothing like most that hit the big screen. The difference? No story, no characters, no romantic or dramatic subplot, just reels and reels of surfing footage.[8] Such pictures are totally committed to *surfing* ... totally.

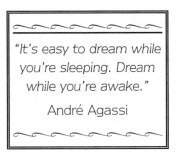

> "It's easy to dream while you're sleeping. Dream while you're awake."
>
> André Agassi

---

[8] Ziolkowski, T. *On a Wave.* New York: Atlantic Monthly Press, 2002.

Back to *High Fidelity.* Ironically, as soon as Rob Gordon recognizes that chronic hedge-betting is the source of his lack of fulfillment and connection—how keeping his options open has only resulted in lost opportunities—his life immediately begins lining up with his dreams.

In short, he stops asking, "Is this the one?" and starts saying, "This *will* be the one." As result of this high fidelity, his relationship with Laura is renewed and intensifies. At the same time, his music business, long languishing and lamely putting along, takes off in a new and exciting direction. As the final credits roll, the potential of both his love and work life, previously dormant, is liberated.

By the way, a new term has entered the American lexicon that attempts to celebrate our collective commitment to nothing: multitasking. In the last few years, speed-doing has eclipsed speed-reading as the measure of the most capable among us. Drive while talking on the cell phone. Conducting business while eating lunch. Watching multiple programs at once by flipping back and forth between channels with your remote. Better yet, watching two programs simultaneously via the in-screen feature on your television!

Believe it or not, someone has actually studied this phenomenon. And while doing two things at once has been heralded as the royal road to efficient and effective living in these complex and demanding times, the research says otherwise. Multitasking actually makes people *less* efficient—especially when the tasks are complicated or unfamiliar.[9] Now, does that description sound remotely similar to life?

In the end, dividing our attention between two activities forces us to belly-ride through both. Sounds like a no-brainer to us. Anyone who has been cut off by someone driving under the influence of a cell phone or munching down a Big Mac® could have told you the same thing with much less time and effort!

---

[9] Smith D. "Multitasking Undermines Our Efficiency, Study Says." *APA Monitor,* 2001, p. 13.

Consider the Erickson family of Firth, Nebraska. In many ways, they were living the American dream. Financially, they were secure.[10] They had all the latest electronic do-dads, a charming home in the countryside, and a beautiful and vivacious young daughter, Mariel. Only one thing was missing. "We didn't have time for each other," fifty-three-year-old father and healthcare administrator Richard recalls. Like many people, they simply felt too rushed—there was just too much going on—for them to enjoy what they had. Worse, taking the time, they all tacitly feared, might cause them to miss out on . . . something.

The typical day started at 5 A.M., when the family bolted out of bed, scarfed down a meager breakfast and a cup of joe, and then rushed out the door. Mary had to drive like crazy in order to get Mariel to day care—thirty miles in the opposite direction from her office—so that she could be back in time to start her job as a lobbyist by 8 A.M.

The process was just as maddening after work, but in the reverse order. Mary would hurry back across the long country roads to fetch Mariel, all the while making contacts and conducting meetings via her cell phone. Following a hurried dinner, Richard barreled down the hall to finish the remodeling job the family had started on their home, and Mary continued to conduct business via the fax machine. What about Mariel? Well, according to her

> "Since the end of World War II, Americans have traveled a path that promised the good life but has left them stuck in a cul-de-sac and feeling unfulfilled."
>
> Ron Grossman

---

[10] Shellenbarger, S. "You Can Find the Time." *Parade Magazine,* Aug. 5, 2001, p. 10.

parents, she began "showing signs of anxiety."

Here are some interesting factoids. In the last few years:

- The average size of a new American home has jumped from 1,500 to 2,129 square feet
- The number of cars has risen from one for every two Americans to one car for each driver
- Sales of vehicles specifically designed for recreational purposes have increased 800 percent
- The number of amusement parks has jumped 300 percent.
- The number of television channels exploded from an average of 10 in the late 1970s to a virtually unlimited number (depending on the type of cable or service one may have)
- According to the latest data, Americans are attending more symphonies, plays, concerts and sporting events than ever before

However, at the same time as opportunities for happiness and contentment have mushroomed:

- The average middle-income, two-parent family is working 660 more hours per year—that's an additional sixteen weeks of work—than in 1979 [11]
- Americans have the least amount of vacation time in the industrialized world [12]
- The average number of times American couples have sex per week is on the decline. (For many, the joy of sex has, apparently, become the job of sex.) [13]
- Time spent together as a family in nonwork and unstructured leisure activities (e.g., eating dinner together, talking) has been waning for several decades

[11] Franklin S. "Running Faster to Fall Further Behind." *Chicago Tribune,* September 15, 2002.

[12] Scheier, L. "Call It a Day, America." *Chicago Tribune,* Health & Family, May 5, 2002. Section 13, p. 1.

[13] Peterson, K. S. "Study Finds Highly Educated Have Less Sex." *USA Today,* January 14, 1998, p. 1.

• A growing body of research shows no increase in feelings of personal or societal contentment in the last fifty years.

"I felt a nagging emptiness," Richard Erickson recalls, in spite of the many blessings the family enjoyed. Rather than a life, the family was always having a "near-life experience." Says Richard, "The time we did spend together was spent on household chores." Mmm. Mmm. Sounds like loads of fun, eh? Makes you want to rush home to the bosom of your family right now.

Anyway, rather than committing to everything and ending up connected to nothing, the couple decided it was time to take a stand, to pop up. The biggest opportunity, they determined, had been staring them in the face all along: their daughter. Richard quit his job to spend more time with Mariel. In order to shorten Mary's commute, the family sold their country home and moved to the city.

> "At the time, I thought, 'Well, somebody should do something about this.' Over time, I realized that somebody was me."
>
> Bill Casey
> (Daughter lost in
> TWA crash in 1975)

Along the way, the stark landscape that had been their life began to blossom. Their home—once merely an office away from the office—began filling with talk and socializing. Over time, Richard and Mary's marriage grew more satisfying. And Mariel? She's fifteen now, and relaxed and happy as ever.

To be sure, we're not saying that "popping up" is easy. Ask any surfer and they will tell you it is a very difficult maneuver. Indeed, most advise practicing on land before ever venturing into the water.

And if you make your way down to the beach early on a Saturday morning, you can usually catch a class of beginners practicing the maneuver on their imaginary surfboards sketched in the sand.

The Erickson family did a "dry run" of sorts when, prior to acting, they spent time reviewing their life, opportunities and priorities.

- What was happening that they'd like to experience more of?
- What would be most fulfilling?
- What was mere fluff, and what was important stuff in their lives?
- What were the steps they could take toward a more meaningful and happy life?

And then they acted.

By the way, if you're stuck trying to figure out when to pop up, the answer is: There is no right time. Unlike positioning, where he who hesitates is lost, staying pressed to the board while life pushes you along will not result in missed opportunities so much as a chronic feeling of something amiss—a burger without the fries, a pizza without the beer, a movie without the popcorn, and so on.

Sure, planning and preparation are good. In most instances, however, you're never likely *to feel* completely ready. So? Just do it. You've already done your homework. The wave has caught and is moving you along. Stand up, and stand up now. In short:

- If not now, when?
- If not this, what?

One more point. We mentioned it at the opening of this chapter, but it bears repeating in the context of popping up. Don't expect to receive a whole lot of support from others for taking a stand. Few will have the same investment in your committing to a course of action as you, whatever your course of action might be: starting a business, taking charge of your finances, developing a healthier lifestyle, getting your spiritual life in order, becoming active in your community, overcoming a destructive habit or attempting to simplify your life. The choices are endless as well as different for each and every one of us.

Most times you'll simply be ignored. In some instances, however, the treatment can be pretty harsh. Remember Robert Reich? He was the Secretary of Labor in the Clinton administration who decided to leave his cabinet position to renew his commitment to his family. Much to his surprise, in acting on this opportunity, he was barraged with a spate of angry letters. "They said my quitting sent a terrible message," he recalls in his book *The Future of Success,* "that a balanced life was not compatible with a high-powered job." He continues, "Others complained that while it was easy for me to leave my job and find another one that paid about as well . . . they didn't have that choice." And still others, he says, "wrote to inform me indignantly that I shouldn't think myself virtuous. Hard work," they lectured him, "was virtuous. Abandoning an important job to spend time with my family was not."[14]

The experience of Reich nicely summarizes the typical arguments levied against popping up and seizing the opportunities before us:

- You *can* have it all so always keep your options completely open
- Nice for a privileged few, but unrealistic for most of us, and
- Stop dreaming and get back to work

To such naysayers, finger-waggers and faultfinders, surfers say, "Bummer. Sorry *you're* having a bad day, dude. Gotta go." And with malice towards none, they pop up and surf away.

And just you wait. Until you've been there, you can't imagine what it's like. We promise that words will barely be able to convey the

---

[14] Reich, R. B. *The Future of Success.* New York: Vintage, 2000.

experience or capture the moment. In reflecting on his choice, for example, Robert Reich merely notes that, "The experience made me notice a lot of things I hadn't seen before." And, in fact, a broader view is precisely what being on top makes possible!

> "Our doubts are traitors and make us lose the good we oft might win by fearing to attempt."
>
> William Shakespeare

Popping up certainly changed our outlook on life. Yes, we had to paddle. And positioning? Oh man, we never thought we'd get the hang of that. What we can say, however, is that being up made all our effort and botched attempts at positioning worth it. Like the line from the old Beach Boys tune goes, we were "sitting on top of the world."

If you're ready to pop up, do it NOW . . . then turn the page.

4

Staying on Top and Keeping the Sand Out of Your Pants

Nature is trying very hard to make us succeed,

but nature does not depend on us.

R. Buckminster Fuller

R iding a wave. It's similar to jetting down the highway in a convertible on a summer afternoon. No, no, it's more like a combination of feelings and experiences. Closer to being totally absorbed in a great flick while simultaneously rappelling down the face of that cliff you scaled moments earlier. Yeah . . . that's more like it. Completely engrossed in that novel you're reading but at the same time plunging, hand on the ripcord of your parachute, hundreds of feet per second toward the Earth.

It's exhilarating and totally captivating, thrilling and completely absorbing. You're fully immersed in the experience, yet also watching and enjoying yourself. At such moments, time collapses and falls by the wayside. You feel invincible, connected, peaceful, exhilarated, contented and together, on top, with-it, resolved, clear-headed, focused and open. You're on a roll. Nothing can stop you. You want to run, shout, clap, dance, hug, share, crank up the radio in your car

A GREAT WAVE REALLY BLOWS YOUR MIND!

and push on the accelerator. It's all of these and more, and it's different for each and every one of us.

At such moments, nothing else matters. All the hassles of daily life—the long commutes, the crabby boss, the endless

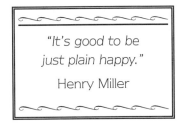

"It's good to be just plain happy."

Henry Miller

bills—any and every annoyance encountered, recede into the background. No matter what has happened before or might take place in the future, regardless of what may be going on around you or in your life, these are the moments that give life that jolt, that zip, that let us know we're not just living, but we're alive!

You don't have to be riding high on a wave right now in order to know what we're talking about. Maybe your life, at this point in time, feels less like the theme from *Rocky,* and more akin to Rachmaninoff's "Isle of the Dead," a gloomy symphony about a deserted island that houses the souls of those forgotten by the living. Take a moment, however, and you're apt to recall these times when life flowed rather than ebbed:

- getting your driver's license
- graduating from school
- falling in love
- closing your first business deal
- seeing the Grand Canyon, the Sistine Chapel or peering over the edge of the Empire State Building
- your baby's birth or first smile

Now imagine all of those events happening at the same time. *That's* what surfers mean by "stoked." Fuel has been added to the fire of life. Heart and soul are stirred into action.

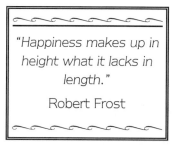

"Happiness makes up in height what it lacks in length."

Robert Frost

Everybody knows such moments. Everyone wants them to continue. Naturally, we all attempt to hold on and extend them as long as possible. Deep down we know full well, however, they will eventually come to an end. And that awareness can either intensify or weaken the experience, propel us to new heights or drive us to the brink (more on this later).

As for surfers, they will tell you there are a few basic skills for making the most of the ride. If you want to stay on top and keep the sand out of your pants, you'll need to know about:

- Footing
- Trimming
- Bailing

Ready? Away we go . . .

Skill Number One: Footing

Pick up a surfboard. Any one will do. Go ahead. Give it the old once over. Look from side to side, from tip to tail. (If you don't have one, look at a picture of one.) Now, do you notice anything that seems even the slightest bit out of the ordinary? Sure, opposite the pointy end it has a fin or two, maybe even three. But that's not what we're hoping to get at. Look again. Is there anything else that strikes you as odd about that sliver of shaped foam and fiberglass? Set the board down and take a step back. Let the whole picture sink in to your consciousness.

Does that help? Yeah, yeah, some wonder if the owner of a laundry might have invented the sport because the surfboard does bear a strange resemblance to an ironing board. Okay, they have a point there. And think about this: You're going to be standing perpendicular on that floating slab of fiberglass while flying at a frightening rate of speed toward the shore.

All right, we give. We'll tell you what we're aiming at. It's the being propelled on *that floating slab of fiberglass* part. Pick up any surfboard and you'll instantly notice there are no safety belts to keep you in place, no little rubber booties riveted to the board in which to insert your feet, no hand or safety rails to hang on to as you are being hurtled toward the shore. Where other sports provide belts, boots, bars, chutes, straps, stirrups and snaps, surfing offers only Newton and his laws of gravity.

Doesn't inspire a great deal of confidence at first glance, does it? Standing upright on a slick slice of polished panel while being propelled "at a frightening rate of speed" with nothing more than some abstract laws of physics to keep you stuck to the board. So, what's the secret?

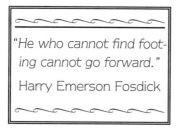

"He who cannot find footing cannot go forward."

Harry Emerson Fosdick

Surfers say: footing. And, while you might not have understood the activities at the time, you've probably seen surfers doing things designed to improve the grip they have on the board. For example? Surfers coat the deck of their boards with a layer of tacky wax. No, the collective "wax on, wax off" movements observed among surfers preparing for the day's rides are not part of some secret ritual hijacked from the *Karate Kid* movies. Rather, it's a dead-serious effort to increase traction, to keep the surfer's feet *connected* with the board. With all this emphasis on connection, you probably won't be surprised to learn that Sex Wax® is one of the bestselling brands. Surfers say: Bond with your board or the board will not stay bonded to you—and you'll suffer the consequences as a result.

Prior to entering the water, surfers also run a hand up and down the length and breadth of their boards. There's almost a sensual quality to the process if you've ever seen it. In spite of how this may look, however, it's not some strange fetish unique to surfers. Rather, they are *attending* to the board, checking for any cracks or fissures

that might compromise its integrity, its ability to support and carry them, buoy them up, for the rides ahead.

Back on land, we would do well to give as much time and attention to footing, in particular, whatever supports and carries us on our journey to the good life. Relationships are an important example. Consider the story of Adolph Stec. For four years, neighbors watched as the once tidy home of this west side resident of Chicago fell into disrepair. Paint chipped and curled, weeds sprung up, and the bushes grew out of control. Although he'd lived in the area for years, no one knew the reclusive old man very well. "He really wasn't a very friendly man," recalled one neighbor. "Not nice at all." Greetings were barely acknowledged with a grunt, if at all.

> "Experience is not what happens to a man. . . . It is a matter of sensibility and intuition, of seeing and hearing the significant things, of paying attention at the right moments."
>
> Aldous Huxley

Every once in a while, someone would try to reach out. They'd make their way up the pathway to his door and knock, but Mr. Stec never answered. "So everyone just went on with their lives," the neighbor said. "He must have abandoned the place, we thought."

"I didn't want the neighborhood to go to pot," said another neighbor. "The grass in his yard got as high as two feet, so for two or three years I mowed his lawn, too." In spite of such efforts, however, the property continued to deteriorate. Mail dwindled and eventually stopped. No forwarding address was ever registered at the post office. Over time, electricity, gas and water were shut off. Workers from the various utility companies were actually sent to the home to

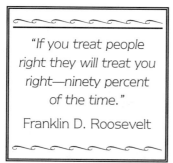

> *"If you treat people right they will treat you right—ninety percent of the time."*
>
> Franklin D. Roosevelt

cut off services at the site.

This state of affairs might have continued indefinitely had the home not been sold to a developer at auction. Mr. Stec had failed to pay his property taxes, had not responded to numerous notices of default sent by the city and did not show up in court on the appointed day to plead his case. His home was then sold. As soon as the new owner opened the door of the residence, however, he immediately understood why. Seated in a chair in the living room of his still fully furnished home was the mummified body of Mr. Stec. By his side was a newspaper dated 1997! He'd been dead for *four years* and no one knew.[15]

Pretty darn gruesome, eh bro? Yeah, and also hard to believe it could happen in our day and age. Even so, you don't have to be Aesop to understand the moral of this story. Bottom line? Fail to attend to your support system and, sooner or later, your support system will fail to attend to you. Is it any surprise, for example, that the handbook created by and for Al Qaeda terrorists explicitly recommended that when infiltrating the country, would-be bombers should move into neighborhoods where people, though living in tight quarters, failed to interact and communicate with one another?

In sum, time and attention, compassion and concern, love and nurturing are the emotional

> *"It is shelter of each other that the people live."*
>
> Irish Proverb

---

[15] McCann, T. "Corpse in House for Up to 4 Years." *Chicago Tribune,* May 10, 2001, p. 1.

glue that keep us connected. And for many of us, whether in our business or our professional lives, connections are what it's all about. That is why surfers wax their boards and make a regular practice of checking for weaknesses. It also explains why surfers wear a "leash"— a small rubber cord connecting the board to the rider's ankle. All such efforts are aimed at improving footing. All help surfers stay bonded to their boards while moving forward in uncertain and rapidly changing conditions.

Skill Number Two: Trimming

Galileo. No, not the guy we mentioned in the last chapter who was put on permanent house arrest for being positioned too far ahead of a breaking wave. Rather, the spacecraft *Galileo* that was launched into space from the bay of the space shuttle in October 1989 on an exploratory mission to the planet Jupiter.

The two-ton satellite was packed with special equipment designed to measure all manner and sorts of cool stuff about our solar system's largest planet: low and high energy-charged particles, cosmic and Jovian dust, as well as planetary magnetic fields. Another section of the craft contained high-resolution cameras for sending back pictures, an infrared and ultraviolet spectrometer to analyze the planet's

atmosphere, and even a device called a photo-polarimeter radiometer that would collect information about radiant and reflected energy. And all of this was powered by a small but potent amount of plutonium.

If you're a fan of *Star Trek,* you'll recall that a similar spacecraft was the reluctant star of the first full-length motion picture based on the original series. In the film, Kirk and crew are sent to investigate a mysterious energy cloud that has cut a swath of destruction through the galaxy and is on a collision course for Earth.

After numerous mishaps along the way, the starship *Enterprise* finally arrives, only to be attacked by the Thing in the cloud. Numerous attempts are made to contact the powerful entity that, by this point in the movie, has taken to calling itself V'ger. For example, Spock ventures out alone in a thruster-equipped space suit and attempts a Vulcan mind-meld with the object.

Eventually, the crew (and viewing audience) learns that the strange cloud-vessel is actually the real-life interplanetary probe *Voyager,* sent into space by NASA in the late 1970s on a mission to explore Jupiter, Saturn, Uranus and Neptune, and then lost. The craft is simply trying to return to Earth in order to fulfill its original purpose: relay the information it has gathered while in space. In the end, the team aboard the starship *Enterprise* manages to outsmart the now self-aware space probe, saving the day and averting the destruction of our planet.

Back on twenty-first-century Earth, scientists smile in amusement at the storyline of the movie. Audience members didn't. The flick was a major bomb at the box office. For the physicists working for NASA, however, the plot was simply too incredible not to laugh. After all, *Voyager, Galileo* and the later satellite, *Cassini,* have less energy onboard than the average car battery. And we're supposed to believe this trickle of juice somehow morphs into a conscious entity with cosmic powers at its disposal? Trekkies say, "Hey, it can happen!" Scientists say, "No way, Roddenberry."

Truth is, the small amount of power that can be packed into such a craft is a major challenge to all space exploration. This is particularly true in getting a rocket off the planet and on its way. Simply put, there is not enough fuel to blast interplanetary probes off Earth and straight to their destination in our solar system. So how do they do

STAR TREK THE MOVIE

IT'S A SCRIPT, JIM, BUT NOT AS WE KNOW IT.

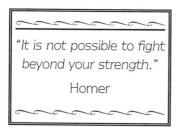

"It is not possible to fight beyond your strength."

Homer

it? In a word, NASA engineers *surf* the craft through space.

Watch surfers in action. They ride *parallel* to the shore rather than pointing their board directly down the face of the wave. Why? Because doing the latter unleashes the power and force of the wave *all at once.* Not only will the ride be shorter, but a wipeout is much more likely—if not inevitable. It's tantamount to scientists trying to build a rocket big enough to contain enough fuel to propel a satellite all the way to its final destination. It boggles the imagination, not to mention the fact that the outcome of such a project is much more likely to be a tremendous explosion than a terrific ride.

Face it, a surfboard has no engine, no plutonium-based propulsion system and no warp drive. In order to ride, surfers must take advantage of the natural properties, the physics of the wave. In short, mindful of the wave's natural gifts, they share in its power and, through their own actions, lend added value to the

"Nature . . . offers all its kingdoms to man as the raw material which he may mold into what is useful."

Ralph Waldo Emerson

wave's energy. In surfing, this process is called "trimming," using one's body weight and footing to exploit the wave's speed and form to the fullest.

As for *Galileo, Voyager* and the other interplanetary probes, aerospace engineers cleverly *used* the gravitational field of a planet to accelerate and alter the course of a spacecraft without having to burn-precious fuel.[16] Basically, the crafts were whipped around a planet and let go, much like a slingshot you would swing around in a circle and then release.[17] Surfers are found in the strangest places, eh?

When it comes to the good life, we are faced with a similar choice: flame out in a quick and furious blaze of glory or exploit the natural properties of whatever opportunity we are riding in order to extend the trip. As an example of the latter, consider

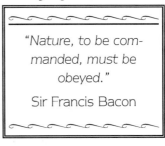

"Nature, to be commanded, must be obeyed."

Sir Francis Bacon

the list below. In particular, look for the qualities shared by the members of this group:

- Paul Newman
- Jennifer Lopez
- Walt Disney
- Jimmy Carter
- Oprah
- Computer Axial Tomography (also known as the CAT scan)

You probably thought you knew the answer until you hit that last item, eh bud? We'll get to the CAT scan in a minute. In the meantime, start with the people first. Sure they're all well-known—but that's not what we're driving at. Rather, everyone on the list has managed to use the opportunities at hand to both enhance and expand their experience of the good life.

For example, actor Paul Newman transformed his screen fame into a line of gourmet food products, the profits from which are

---

[16] *www.resa.net/nasa/mechanics.htm.*
[17] *www.windows.ucar.edu/tour/link=/kids_space/gravity_ assist.html.*

>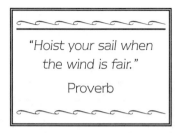
>
> *"Hoist your sail when the wind is fair."*
>
> Proverb

donated to charity. Even if not intentional, Newman's Own has served to increase his prominence and notoriety! For her part, Jennifer Lopez goes from the silver screen to become one of the most popular, if not *the* most popular, female singers of the last decade. Watch out Kmart and Kathy Ireland, because J. Lo's revealing—if not controversial—fashion sense will most certainly lead to a clothing line bearing more than her name.

Then there's Walt Disney. By now, almost every person on the planet recognizes the image of Mickey Mouse. The Midwestern-born entrepreneur didn't stop there. Rather, he surfed his original forty-dollar investment and simple, black-and-white cartoon character into a worldwide entertainment empire that now includes motion-picture studios, theme parks, clothing and product lines, and media outlets.

As for Jimmy Carter, following what many consider a largely undistinguished term as president of the United States, the former peanut farmer from Plains, Georgia, parlayed the momentum from the Middle East peace accords into a worldwide peacemaking

campaign that eventually won him worldwide acclaim and the Nobel Peace Prize. And Oprah? This amazing woman managed to turn an appearance on a local morning program into the longest running and most popular talk show in television history, an acting career, and turns as a nationwide book-club leader, magazine publisher, self-help and weight-loss guru, and cable and internet media mogul. Oh yeah, and philanthropist! Over the years, she's also devoted lots of time and millions of dollars to a variety of charitable activities.

All told, once these successful people were up and riding, they didn't just sit back and rest on their laurels. Rather, like surfers, they used their weight and footing to trim in and out, up and down, and back and forth across the wave they were riding.

Still wondering what this illustrious group has in common with the CAT scan? Well, we have to admit it's rather oblique. There is a connection, however. *The Beatles.* That's right, the rock band that hasn't recorded a song

"Make hay while the sun shines."

Proverb

in more than three decades but managed to have a hit album *(The Beatles 1)* in the year 2000. Here it is: The lads from Liverpool were among the earliest and most important investors in the emerging medical-imaging technology, thereby extending their ride into new and uncharted territories.

Skill Number Three: Bailing

Catch a wave, and you're sitting on top of the world. Ride it all the way into shore and . . . you'll end up with sand in your pants, for sure. We promise. Guaranteed. It'll be a gritty experience the likes of which you'll never forget. Moreover, since the water at the shore is always moving *out,* you can soon expect to be going backward rather than forward into the surf. That is, at least until you're smashed from behind by the next incoming set of waves and rolled about, to and fro, in the foam. You guessed it: more sand.

A young surfer once asked Surfmaster, "When you are finally standing on the board and riding the wave, what should you do next?" Without hesitation, the wise old advisor responded, "Why, step off the board, of course."

As paradoxical as this may sound, "bailing" out of a wave before it crumbles into nothing actually makes it possible for surfers to stay on top *longer.* How? you might ask. By positioning them closer to the *next* set of waves. Plus, a surfer who doesn't have to paddle all the way back out to the line-up from the shore won't tire out as quickly. Do the math: Less time spent recuperating equals more time for riding. Best of all, the sand churned up in the sloppy soup at the shore is completely avoided.

Nonetheless, once you're riding high, the temptation to do everything to maintain the ride for as long as possible *on that particular wave* becomes quite strong. We talk, for example, about "milking an opportunity for all it's worth," "mining that

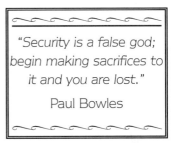

"Security is a false god; begin making sacrifices to it and you are lost."

Paul Bowles

vein until it's tapped out" and "squeezing blood from a stone." Surfers know, however, that, in spite of their efforts, the average ride lasts but a few seconds (around fifteen to twenty). In fact, a minute qualifies as a super long run in the sport!

In the same way, most opportunities in life are relatively short-lived. We hope we'll always be in love, that our children will forever be our kids, that our jobs, the economy and the world will remain stable. And yet, most of us know that, no matter how sure our footing or apt our trim, all things eventually come to an end. Spring gives way to summer, children grow into adults, and youth invariably gives way to old age.

On that note, consider the following story. A woman dies and goes to heaven. When she meets St. Peter at the pearly gates to check in, he informs her that a mistake has been made. "It's not your time," he says. "You have many, many more years to live." In the weeks following this experience, the woman undergoes extensive plastic surgery. She has a facelift, tummy tuck, liposuction and boob job. "If I'm going to live so long," she reasons, "I might as well look good—

at least as good as I did when I was in my youth."

Not long thereafter, the woman is run down by a car and killed while crossing a street. Confused and angry, she storms to the pearly gates and pounds loudly. When St. Peter answers, the woman can barely contain herself. "I thought you said I had many more years to live," she fumes. St. Peter is momentarily bewildered. He looks at the

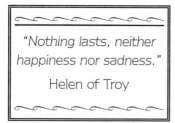

"Nothing lasts, neither happiness nor sadness."

Helen of Troy

woman, blinks his eyes a couple of times and scratches his head. "Oh my," he finally responds, "is that *you?*"

The point? Try to hang on to what you have and you'll miss the opportunities that are breaking now. Plus, you'll end up stuck at the

FACE IT, DUDE—
YOU'RE TENDING
TO HANG ON JUST
A LITTLE TOO
LONG.

shoreline picking sand out of your shorts and reminiscing about the "good old days" with the rest of life's tourists. By the way, nostalgia is not just a fond memory. It's also a feeling of loss—the feeling that what you once had, you'll never have again. Surfers say: bag that. *There will always be another wave.*

Nowhere is the brevity of opportunity more apparent nowadays than in the world of work. Job insecurity has replaced job security in the present economy. Unlike the previous generation, few of us can expect to receive the proverbial gold watch for long and loyal service. Indeed, if current trends are any indication, most of us will end our work lives in entirely different careers. For example, in her book *Successful Recareering,* author and consultant Joyce A. Schwartz cites sources indicating that the average American should prepare to change careers seven times during their lifetime. That's careers mind you—not jobs.[18] Unless you're near retirement and can ride your current position all the way into shore, workers in the modern job market must be prepared to kick out of whatever wave they are riding—however impressive, fun or enduring it may be at the moment.

Musician and performance artist David Bowie is one person who clearly understands the importance of "stepping off the board" long before the wave he's riding peters out. The career of this icon of popular music began with his birth as David Robert Jones in the working-class neighborhood of Brixton, England. Like other kids growing up in the 1960s, he listened to rock and roll and dreamed of someday hitting it

> "Only in growth, reform and change paradoxically enough is true security to be found."
>
> Anne Morrow Lindbergh

---

[18] Schwartz, J.A. *Successful Recareering,* Hawthorn, N.J.: Career Press, 1993, p. 11.

big with his own band. These were heady times for the new musical import from America, and Little Richard and Fats Domino were among the young Brit's favorites.

He began seriously pursuing his own dream at age fifteen! His first band, *The Conrads,* played the pop tunes of the day, but they went nowhere. His second group, *Davey Jones and the King Bees*, even recorded a single. Nevertheless, it, along with the band, soon disappeared.

As the Beatles were riding a wave of popularity that carried the foursome all the way to America, seventeen-year-old David was picking up with his third band, *The Manish Boys*. The group managed to get some media attention by forming The Society for the Prevention of Cruelty to Long Haired Men. The interest was short-lived, however, and the group soon disbanded.

David continued paddling as the wave of rock and roll grew in size and influence. The British group The Rolling Stones burst onto the scene. Other groups quickly followed, first becoming popular in the U.K. and then being propelled across the Atlantic to the golden shores of success in America.

Meanwhile, David worked feverishly to position himself in front of the wave. He changed his last name to Bowie when an album by future Monkees lead singer Davey Jones made its way up the British charts. As David Bowie, he released his first single. He signed with famed showbiz manager Ken Pitt—a man who successfully steered the careers of Frank Sinatra and Judy Garland. In quick succession, he released his first solo album, took up acting, got some radio play, won an award for one of his songs at an international music festival and even released a second album!

In spite of all his hard work, however, the wave simply failed to catch and move Bowie's career along. His albums sold poorly, his songs disappeared from the radio very quickly, and his acting career stalled. At the same time, audience members heckled his latest band, a wildly costumed, makeup-wearing group known as *The Hype*, off the stage. At age twenty-two, it appeared that David Bowie's ride was over before it ever really started.

And then suddenly, success struck. Bowie signed with RCA. His first album, *Hunky Dory*, contained the song, "Changes," which got a modest amount of airtime in the United States and became something of a hit. When his next record, *The Rise and Fall of Ziggy Stardust and the Spiders from Mars*, was released, his popularity soared and Bowie was propelled to super stardom.

> "Boldness,
> more boldness,
> and always boldness."
>
> George Jacques Danton

As the line from the title track of the album goes, "Wam bam, thank you, Ma'am!" Bowie's androgynous, gender-bending persona and penchant for cross-dressing acted as the perfect trim, keeping him on the cutting edge of rock and roll by causing a major public stir. Kids bought his records by the millions. Grown-ups reacted with fear and concern. Ultimately, the British rocker's unique mixture of music, fashion and performance launched the era of glam rock and paved the way for later groups as diverse as Queen and Kiss. His music and image even inspired a play that bombed on Broadway but was made into a movie that became a cult classic. Recall *The Rocky Horror Picture Show*?

At age twenty-five, Bowie was riding high. His next LP, *Aladdin Sane*, quickly went to number one. He embarked on a world tour, crisscrossing the globe on a wave of international popularity that carried him to the United States, Japan, Russia and England. In each city, he played to sold-out houses. Where just a few years earlier, his music was ignored, he now had five albums in the top forty—three in the top fifteen! Never before in the history of rock and roll had a solo artist achieved such success.

> *"To change one's life;*
> *start immediately,*
> *do it flamboyantly.*
> *No exceptions."*
>
> William James

So what did Bowie do at this point? At age twenty-six—just a year and a half into his meteoric ride to the top—he announced his retirement. Simply put, *he stepped off the board*. No, this was not some cheap publicity stunt. Bowie was dead serious: no more Ziggy, no more Spiders from Mars. He was through. Needless to say, his fans were shocked and surprised. Popular rumor suggested he would soon be another member of the One-Hit-Wonder Club. For his part, however, Bowie was establishing a pattern that would both guide and sustain his musical career over the next three decades: constant change.

One can hardly argue with his success. Since the demise of Ziggy, Bowie has wowed legions of fans with a series of new musical styles and innovative performances. For example, in his very next album, *Pin Ups,* he revisited the mid-1960s British rock scene known as Mersey sound. After that, he released *Diamond Dogs,* an attempt at a rock opera based on Orwell's futuristic novel about totalitarianism, *1984.* While the musical never got off the ground, the album contained what would become two rock and roll classics, "Rebel, Rebel" and "1984." With the aid of Luther Vandross, his 1975 release entitled *Young Americans* experimented with rhythm and blues. "Fame," written and performed with John Lennon, became his first number-one song in the United States.

A completely transformed Bowie once again greeted the music-buying public on the 1976 record, *Stationtostation.* Gone were the feminine clothing, spiked red hair and space-age makeup. In their place was a mature, clean-cut and elegantly dressed figure that would serve as a role model to many bands popular in the 1980s. The album contained the hit "Golden Years" and became his highest charting since the release of *Diamond Dogs.*

> "There's no security on this Earth; there's only opportunity."
>
> Douglas MacArthur

We could go on and on. Whether trying to break free of the stranglehold that disco music had on late 1970s music with his ultramodern album *Low* and the subsequent but similar sounding *Lodger* and *Heroes,* or embracing mainstream pop music with his chart-topping dance compilation, *Let's Dance,* Bowie has never chosen to ride any particular wave very far before bailing. Sure he's had some failures along the way. The albums *Scarey Monsters (and Super Creeps), Tonight,* and *Never Let me Down,* among others, never quite took off. (That's a nice way of saying they bombed.) He also made several movies along the way that went nowhere (e.g., *Labyrinth, The Man Who Fell to Earth, The Hunger* and *Absolute Beginners*).

But he kept at it, and at age fifty-five, Bowie is one of the most enduring and successful musicians in history. Last year, he released his twenty-seventh studio album, *Heathen.* Oh yeah, did we mention that he's married to supermodel Iman, has a new child, has homes in four countries, is worth an estimated billion dollars and was recently inducted into the Rock and Roll Hall of Fame? He's also a person who knows intimately that the good life is an act of faith, the experience of which is in the leap, not the destination.[19]

Here's another way of looking at the whole idea of bailing while the going is still good. Every fall, the new television season starts with a crop of fresh programs vying for public attention. The competition is fierce. From week to week, network execs pore over the Nielsen ratings attempting to separate the wheat from the chaff. In the end, only a handful of the programs that started the season are renewed. The

---

[19] *A&E Biography: David Bowie.* Twentieth-Century Fox Film Corporation, 2002.

rest are consigned to the dustbin of boob-tube history. Who remembers *Coronet Blue* or *Time Tunnel,* for example?

Of the shows that do remain, only a small number go on to attract a nationwide audience and hit superstar status. Programs such as *I Love Lucy, All in the Family, The Andy Griffith Show, Gilligan's Island,* even *The Brady Bunch,* immediately come to mind. So popular are these programs that calls for a reunion show often begin as soon as the original series goes out of production—a temptation that has, over the years, led to many disappointing results.

Archie's Place never came close to the cutting-edge social commentary of *All in the Family. The Lucy and Ricky Show* had all of the characters but none of the charm or humor of the original series, and the three made-for-television *Gilligan's Island* specials would frankly have been better off had they been left stranded on a deserted island with the rest of the original cast. The Brady family reunions were perhaps most dreadful of all. Suffice it to say, the cast would probably have been better off had they stayed where many of them apparently ended up—on the Love Boat.

Surfers say, "You can't ride the same wave twice." Sure, many of us try. And when the going is (or has been) good, the temptation to hang on is strong. So *very* strong. Only a fool would wish away the overwhelming feelings of passion that accompany the start of an intimate relationship, for example. Make such feelings the basis of your love life, however, and you'll only end up frustrated and lonely. For a relationship to last, passion must give way to companionship, companionship eventually transform into partnership, and once the family is reared and the children have left the nest, partnership must open up to renewal and regeneration. Such is the pattern of life. There simply is no respite from *change.* Nature's message: evolve or die.

Even when riding high, when you've mastered the skills of footing, trimming and bailing, you are likely to encounter forces that can keep you off the board. No worries, it's part of surfing. In the next chapter, we give you a heads-up on the obstacles you're most likely to encounter as well as some tips for handling them.

Dealing with Bad Weather, Poor Surfing Conditions and Wipeouts

Life is not the way it's supposed to be.
It's the way it is. The way you cope with it
is what makes the difference.

Virginia Satir

It's inevitable. You can't stop it, no matter what you do. You wake up in the morning fresh from a night spent dreaming about the breakers and stoked for a day at the beach. Then you hear the sound, muted at first, but building. You run to the nearest window, push the slats of the blinds apart, and your worst suspicions are confirmed: wind, rain, and dreary, overcast skies. The weather stinks.

> "Nature has no mercy at all. Nature says, 'I'm going to snow. If you have on a bikini and no snowshoes, that's tough. I am going to snow anyway.'"
>
> Maya Angelou

Or how about this? You've been planning a surfing trip for a long time. You've studied and prepared, scoping out the best spots and collecting all the right equipment. The time has finally arrived. You pack your threads and gear and make your way to the beach. As you crest the last dune, board in hand, you catch your first glimpse of the ocean—the surf is knee-high mush, flat. You're totally skunked.

What to do? Unlike staying at home, comfortably positioned in front of your PS2™ or Xbox™, surfing is a real-life, real-time proposition. You can't change the disk or open the options screen to alter the game conditions or level of difficulty. What's more, you can't use the cheat guides you downloaded last night from the Internet to stack the outcome in your favor. Here now, today, at the beach, nature rules—just as it has for the past five or six billion years the planet's been around. And the

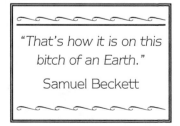

> "That's how it is on this bitch of an Earth."
>
> Samuel Beckett

ocean, one of the most powerful and dynamic forces on Earth, cares not a wit about what you or anybody else thinks or wants.

If that were not enough, thanks to whoever Murphy is or was, we're stuck with his law. You know, the old maxim that "whatever can go wrong, *will*." Count on it. So . . . imagine this . . . you're about to catch your connecting flight to Hawaii for that long-awaited vacation. After putting up with hours of delay and time in the air, departure is now just minutes away. You're nearly there. The last leg. You can almost hear the waves breaking, almost taste the salty ocean air.

You start the boarding check and something about the way you look (or just dumb luck) earns you the sudden, undivided attention of the security people. Tired, tense and a little too short on your fuse, *it* slips out—a stupid remark. You thought nobody heard you, but misfortune smiles once more. "Sir, would come this way?" You follow. "May we look through your bag?" You nod. "Will you take off your shoes?" You sigh and comply.

Meanwhile, standing barefoot under the pale light of the overhead fluorescent fixture with all the other security rejects, you hear the announcement. "Final call for Flight 123 to Oahu." And nobody, least of all the security guard who's passing the buzzing wand between your legs, gives a flying leap about your vacation.

As visions of your long hoped-for trip slowly evaporate, you begin searching for some way to expedite the process. You look around, step briefly out of and then back into line. That cinches it as far as security is concerned. They'd like to spend

> "The foolish reject what they see, not what they think; the wise reject what they think, not what they see."
>
> Huang Po

some "special time" with you . . . if you wouldn't mind coming this way, sir. Bye-bye, Hawaii. Hello, heartache. No surfing for you in the foreseeable future.

To the casual observer or wannabe, bad weather, bad surf and bad luck simply don't happen to surfers. After all, surfing is now part of American mythology. Just as cowboys "never hear a discouraging word" and "the skies are not cloudy all day," surfers are supposed to enjoy great sun, warm water and perfect surf. It's always a great day at the beach—at least, that's how it always looks in the beach-blanket flicks.

Seasoned surfers say, "Bogus!" Good surfing days run neck and neck with lousy ones. What's up comes down, the yin has its yang, night follows day, and, as we made clear in the last chapter, all good things come to an end. That's the fact, Jack. Simply put, surfing, like life, has its share of obstacles and impediments, stuff that puts a good ride an arm's length (or sometimes more) away. Over the years, we've found they boil down to three big ones:

- Weather (mostly the bad kind)
- Poor surfing conditions
- Wipeouts

Here's what we've found about each condition and, more importantly, what surfers do to keep their heads when everything conspires to make bad your day at the beach.

Weather (Mostly the Bad Kind)

Weather \'we-[th]&r\ *n* [origin: Middle English *weder*, before 12th century] (1) The general atmospheric condition as regards temperature, moisture, winds, or other meteorological phenomena; (2) state or vicissitude of life or fortune.

Bad weather \'bad 'we-[th]&r\ *n* [origin: *Scott, Mark & Seth*] (1) (and only one). Any of the above you don't like.

In addition to love, kids, work and, yes, sex, no subject is more bandied about than the weather. It is an international preoccupation. Whole vocabularies have arisen to describe its moods and effects. Weather-bitten, weather-bleached, weather-driven, weather-sick, weather-bound, weather-tight

"A great, great deal has been said about weather, but very little has ever been done."

Mark Twain

and, of course, under the weather are just a few of the words or phrases we invoke in daily conversation. If you can't get enough of the weather by simply looking out your window or standing outside, then by goodness, you can check the weather report in the newspaper, call the National Weather Service, go to any number of exclusively weather-oriented Web sites, tune in to the Weather Channel on cable, or wait for the local evening news to quit the teasers every five minutes and give you the real scoop on tomorrow's weather.

The weather is often the primary way humans seem to break the ice in conversation. "So what do you think about this weather we're having?" "Have you heard the latest forecast?" "Feels pretty cold [hot,

warm, humid, etc.] for this time of year." Furthermore, if you're stuck on what to say to anybody in a long-distance conversation, you can always ask, "How's the weather there?" Geez!

Naturally, we're obsessed with the weather because it can be a big deal. It can make the day one to remember—a Kodak moment—or put the big kibosh on your best-made plans. For some, it is a maker or breaker. If you don't believe that, spend a few minutes talking to a farmer or two. Wet, dry, cold and hot spells dog their every step. When the weather's good, it makes nearly everyone happy. When bad, it carries the potential of becoming a major obstacle, one of the four horsemen of the agricultural apocalypse.

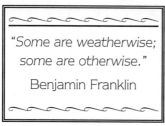

"Some are weatherwise; some are otherwise."

Benjamin Franklin

Like farmers, surfers work hard to understand the weather. They have to—the very act of surfing depends on it. They get weather-wise through long and careful observation, and by checking out Web-based beach cams, listening to local surf reports and tapping into ongoing chat on the surfing grapevine (also known as gossip). Over time, they learn the particular characteristics and quirks of weather by the ocean.

For instance, perched on their boards waiting for the incoming set, surfers quickly become acquainted with the relationship between the wind and the waves. In this timeless process, waves are whipped up by the wind when air turbulence creates little pockets of low and high pressure that suck and push on the water. The size of the wave—an important consideration for surfers—depends on the wind's strength, the duration of the blow and the "fetch," that is, how far it blows over the water. Simply put, more fetch equals more energy transmitted to the water that, in turn, translates into more waves.[20] Pretty fetchen cool, eh?

There's more. Surfers also understand that good surfing waves come about through a complex interplay of local and offshore weather systems that differ in their intensity and distance from the surf break. Here's the way it works. Let's say a storm occurs fifty to five hundred miles offshore. Its intensity is medium, generating winds gusting between thirty-five and forty-five knots. The storm lasts a few days, and the fetch is also medium. At the shore it is sunny and clear with light offshore winds, blowing from land to sea. The expected payoff: The medium storm generates good-sized waves, and the local weather makes for a perfect day in the surf. The light offshore winds act to groom and fashion the waves into a bodacious shape.[21]

So what's the point of all this meteorological minutiae? As para-doxical as it may sound, appreciating the weather's powerful and broad-reaching role in wave for-mation enables surfers to main-tain a *larger* perspective. It reminds them of the importance of keeping the big picture in mind when assessing today's and antici-pating tomorrow's conditions.

As the information shows, the

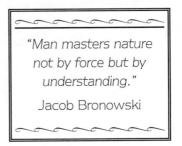

"Man masters nature not by force but by understanding."

Jacob Bronowski

---

[20] Cosgrove, B. *Eyewitness Books: Weather,* New York: Knopf, 2000, p. 57.

[21] *www.discovery.com/news/features/surfing/perfectwave.html.*

ocean and weather are so interconnected that events taking place hundreds (even thousands) of miles away can have a tremendous impact on local surf. What you see before you is the final outcome of forces far beyond your immediate perception (and control). Therefore, to fully understand *your* surf, you always need to be mindful of what is happening beyond your immediate horizon.

In many ways, it is the same for the good life. Keeping the big picture in mind can save us from being shortsighted regardless of current weather conditions. Consider what has taken place over the last decade in the rearing of our children. In 1996, more than six hundred thousand prescriptions for Prozac™—a powerful psychiatric drug—were written for kids under the age of eighteen. More than two hundred thousand of those scripts were for children between six and twelve, three thousand for infants less than a year old.[22] Never mind that the drug had yet to be approved by the FDA for use with kids *under any circumstances.* In fact, seven out of ten drugs given to children have never been tested and proven safe or effective for use by them. So what's happening here? Is depression reaching epidemic proportions in our children?

> "Surfing is good for the soul; worries seems to drift away as you scan the horizon for the next wave."
>
> Ed Daley

Hardly. Instead, in wanting to do right, many of us have been enjoined to go over the top. For instance, a difficulty or situation that otherwise a child would naturally outgrow, we're told now requires the psychiatric equivalent of a first strike. *Perspective is discouraged.* In its place, we're told to "nip this baby in the bud."

---

[22] Duncan, B.L. and Miller, S.D. *The Heroic Client.* San Francisco: Jossey-Bass, 2000.

Not all that long ago, parents consulted a member of the extended family—mother, father, grandparent, trusted aunt or sibling—or a trusted friend, pastor or mentor when they found some aspect of their child's behavior troublesome. Experiences were shared. Common sense was dispensed. To wit, "Just sit tight. Don't worry. *It's a phase.* You did the same thing when you were that age." Or, "This is what we did. Give it a go." Others wisely advised, "Just ignore it. It'll pass."

Of course, that's not to say that such advice was always right. It's clear from the largely positive results, however, that generations of American children successfully survived the ups and downs of growing up without having to be medicated.

> "Trouble brings experience, and experience brings wisdom."
>
> Anonymous

Put another way, parents of the past understood the vicissitudes of weather. They somehow knew and trusted that storms in their children's behavior would come and go, that low-pressure fronts would soon be followed by high-pressure ones, and that dull or dark days would eventually yield to sunny. Today's parents, by contrast, have somehow been convinced that the perspective of parents past is outdated and naïve—that each blip on the weather radar requires the expert machinations of a rainmaker to avoid a drought in adulthood. How otherwise can one explain the dramatic increase in the number of kids being diagnosed with attention deficit disorder? Indeed, a third of American boys are now considered abnormal![23] Either a plague has hit the country or Chicken Little has been put in charge of the classroom.

Keeping the big picture firmly in mind can provide real-life, real-time dividends. For surfers, tracking the larger weather systems gives valuable information as to when the local surf will be primo. For all of us, paying attention to the whole context ensures that our worries stay in proportion and keep close pace with reality. While on the subject of kids, for example, consider the rash of child abductions that struck the country during the summer of 2002. First, Elizabeth Smart

---

[23] D. McGuiness in Fisher, S. and Greenberg, R. (eds.). *The Limits of Biological Treatments for Psychological Distress.* 1989, pp. 151–187.

was kidnapped in Utah (and not found until March 2003). Then, five-year-old Samantha Runnion was snatched from her doorstep and later found murdered. Erica Pratt was next, taken from her Philadelphia row house and held in a basement for days before managing to escape on her own. Weeks later, another girl, six-year-old Casey Williamson, disappeared in Missouri and was later found dead.

Everyone wondered what was happening in our fine land. Clearly, it seemed that the country was in the grips of an epidemic. We were glued to our televisions, watching anguished parents, listening to the advocates and experts. Only a totally disconnected or completely heartless person could have avoided feeling some measure of panic and fear. It was palpable. Parents everywhere became more vigilant, keeping closer tabs on their kids and looking out for the latest Amber Alert. And while one cannot come close to imagining the pain and suffering of those whose children had been taken, the truth is that the actual number of the stranger abductions has been steadily declining, making the summer of 2002 one of the safest on record.[24]

In addition to offering perspective, anyone who watches the weather also learns to appreciate change. Good can rapidly flip-flop with bad. It is dynamic with a capital "D." What makes for bad surfing weather today may yield better results tomorrow (and vice versa). Storms come and go, and the wind is a fickle friend. For these reasons, the watchwords are: stay frosty (alert), stay informed (watch and listen to the forecasts) and never confuse the transitory with the permanent. In fact, it is the changeableness of the weather that gives rise to hope as well as adding excitement and spice to life's enchilada. Surfers know to presuppose or pretend that the weather is something other than what it is—a sure and fast ride to anything but the good life.

---

[24] Goodman, E. "Danger Doesn't Equal Reality in Child Abductions." *The Oregonian,* Aug. 8, 2002.

Sure, back on shore we *know* that weather changes. Who doesn't? Yet, sometimes we forget this important fact with unfavorable results. Check this out. Stena Daniels was born in Iceland in the late 1800s. Two weeks after her birth, her mother died. Unable to care for the newborn and tend to the other children, Stena's father gave his only daughter up for adoption. Numerous other hardships followed. At the tender age of eight, Stena became deathly ill with scarlet fever. Though she survived, she permanently lost hearing in both ears.

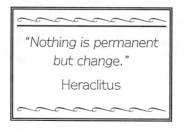

"Nothing is permanent but change."

Heraclitus

Eventually, Stena immigrated to the United States with her adoptive family. Together, they pioneered their way across the country, eventually settling in the west and becoming farmers. In time, she married and started a family of her own. Then, in 1929, her life took another fateful turn. Along with many other Americans, Stena and her husband Clarence lost their entire life savings during a run on their bank in the aftermath of the stock-market collapse.

In spite of having already survived much misfortune, the deprivation that accompanied the Great Depression left a permanent mark

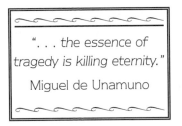

". . . the essence of tragedy is killing eternity."

Miguel de Unamuno

on Stena. She vowed *never* to put her faith (or money) in a bank again. Never. And for the next five decades of her long life, she kept her promise, secreting her increasing wealth in various spots around the house and on her farm. To this day, her grandchildren can still remember her asking them to wait while she disappeared into an adjoining room to fetch a silver dollar from one of her many secret hiding places.

Almost everyone knows that the stock market has faithfully returned 10 to 11 percent on investments since those fateful days in October 1929. Had Stena invested her money in the market in spite of her experience, the entire family would now be on easy street. Unfortunately, in her mind, once the banking industry had collapsed, that was it. The market could never be trusted to yield anything but disaster. Simply put, she mistook a temporary change in the financial weather as the forecast for the rest of her life. As a result, following her death, surviving family members found themselves having to turn the house and property inside out to find her savings. Despite a Herculean effort, they still do not know whether they completely recovered her stash.

Researchers have examined the human penchant for making the transient permanent. In 1967, Martin Seligman and S. F. Maier of the University of Pennsylvania conducted a seminal experiment. They first subjected dogs to electric shocks they could not escape.

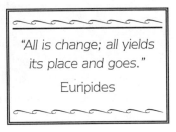

"All is change; all yields its place and goes."

Euripides

As you can expect, the dogs had a very hard time with this. They first barked, yelped and jumped about. Eventually, however, they gave up, laying down in defeat, barely moving when the electricity was turned on.

In the next phase of the study, the very same dogs were placed in a device called a shuttle box. Unlike the original scenario, this apparatus made it possible for the animals to move from one part of the box to another in order to escape the shocks. Technically, therefore, they were no longer trapped as they had been in the first part of the study. The electric shock was then administered again.

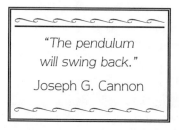

"The pendulum will swing back."

Joseph G. Cannon

Contrary to what one might expect (and hope), the animals did *not* move to escape. Instead, they remained passive, bearing the shocks in silence. Some dogs never learned to escape, even when the experimenters physically moved them to the next compartment. By converting a painful, short-lived, aversive experience into a life sentence, the dogs had learned to be helpless. Scientists have used these and other similar findings to explain how people become depressed, thus losing hope for the good life.[25]

Along these same lines, it is hard to imagine how anyone in what NBC anchorman Tom Brokaw labeled the "Greatest Generation" could ever conceive of a good life.[26] After living through the Great Depression, they faced history's most massive and destructive war. Okay, you're right, we won. Nevertheless, the nation endured the surprise attack on Pearl Harbor, the near-total decimation of the Pacific fleet, the fall of the Philippines and the damnable Bataan Death

[25] Johnson, L., and Miller, S. D. "Modification of Depression Risk Factors: A Solution-Focused Approach." *Psychotherapy, 31,* (2), 1994, 244–253.

[26] Brokaw, T. *The Greatest Generation,* New York: Random House, 1998.

March. In very short order, the weather turned mighty ugly and looked like it was settling in to be a long and bitter stationary front.

> *"The purest ore is produced from the hottest furnace, and the brightest thunderbolt is elicited from the darkest storm."*
>
> Charles Caleb Colton

For the military and civilian population, the shock of Pearl Harbor and the continuing shocks coming from numerous defeats in battle made for many dark days. Fear, grief, rage and uncertainty were but a few of the stormy feelings. The Axis powers looked like an unstoppable juggernaut, which our forces—unprepared and in disarray—were helpless to stop. The experience was so compelling that Baby Boomers will tell you that World War II was like a permanent houseguest. It was invited to the dinner table, encouraged many a sober reminiscence and conversation, and never wandered too far out the door.

Despite the war's capacity to yield despair, our parents and grandparents didn't give up. No whimpering dogs in a cage here. In their hearts they knew this was a temporary downturn and that, once again, the weather would change. They showed their enemies what for and, when it was over, came home and created the most productive and powerful economy the world has ever seen. Pretty amazing, eh? Especially when you contrast that with some of the stuff we complain about today.

This reminds us of a Surfmaster story. One day, the wise old surfer was sitting on the beach in the rain. And brother, was it raining! Everything was coming down: cats, dogs, lions, tigers and bears. Waves were breaking ferociously, smashing the shore with

the sound of thunder. Nobody dared ride in this squall; that is, nobody who wanted to live another day.

At that point, two young novices passed by. The first blurted out, "Look at this. The day is *totally* wrecked." The second then quickly chimed in, "Yeah . . . *totally*. Might as well go home; there's nothing here for us." Fixing his knowing gaze on the two, the Surfmaster first smiled broadly and then said, "Drink it up, boys. It's liquid pineapple. Tomorrow, all there will be is constant sunshine." The novices looked at each other, dumbfounded. Together, they joined Surfmaster sitting on the sand and toasting their good fortune.

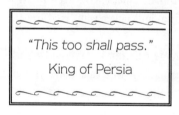

"This too shall pass."

King of Persia

Poor Surfing Conditions

Closely related to weather—and talked about nearly as often—are poor surfing conditions. To some extent, what qualifies for lousy surf is influenced by each surfer's idea of what constitutes a perfect wave. If your little slice of heaven is a peeling point-break of about two to ten feet tall that seems to go on forever (visit Rincon near Carpinteria,

California), anything that falls outside of that zone will be a drag. If your preference is for "killers," like the breakers routinely found at a surf spot off Todos Santos Island, near Baja, Mexico, anything other than a four-story, roaring momboosa (massive,

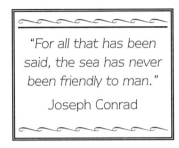

"For all that has been said, the sea has never been friendly to man."

Joseph Conrad

monstrous) will leave you feeling lame. Of course, nearly all surfers agree that cresting that last dune after a long trek through the bush only to find a glassy ocean is a bummer. In this case, a strong onshore wind, blowing from sea to land, gives the water the appearance of glass. More to the point, however, a glassy ocean means no waves. No waves at all.[27]

Fortunately, poor surfing conditions are surmountable because the surf is always up someplace. The obvious solution? Pick up your board, trek back through the bush, and once you're on the main road again, walk, thumb, ride or drive your way to the next beach. Look at it this way: If you're perched on your board complaining about the local conditions, you're not really surfing anyway. In fact, one of the little tortures surfers inflict on themselves is to say, "Around the corner or on the other side of the planet, there's a wave breaking right now better than the one in front of me."[28] Surfers say: Grab your board by the rails and move along, little gremmie!

One place in life where the surf has been especially poor of late is the stock market. There's no need to rehash the bad news in any detail here. Suffice it to say, the year 2000 found most U.S. and foreign stocks in the red. Many—including ourselves—saw our

---

[27] *www.discovery.com/news/features/surfing/physics.html.*
[28] Ibid.

investments in the good life—early retirement and relocation to our favorite surfing spots—vanish into thin air.

Despite the dismal results, financial planners, mutual-fund managers and talking heads remain in agreement. "Stay the course," they advise. "Don't jump ship." Rather, "Be in the market for the long term and don't put your eggs in one basket." This common adage is known as "diversification" and "asset allocation" in financial-speak.

> "This deceptively simple formula, more of the same, is one of the most effective recipes for disaster that has gradually evolved on our planet."
>
> Paul Watzlawick

You increase your net worth, the accepted wisdom goes, by spreading your investments among a variety of holdings and then waiting. At the end of the year, what gains you make are an average of your winners and losers.

Now, here's how this strategy sounds to your average surfer. Every day one surfer goes out to his favorite stretch of ocean and catches every wave that breaks. Nearby, another surfer at a different beach catches none. Average the performance of the two surfers together, however, and the result is that each rode 50 percent of the waves that day. Sounds good, unless you are the surfer who, in spite of the numbers, caught no waves at all.

Clearly, the place that yields no waves, that part of the ocean, is not the place to park your board. Stay there, and you won't surf. It's as simple as that. And as far as averages are concerned, when the surfing conditions are poor, it's a gonzo waste of time and effort, a bad strategy. Get in your van and go where you can catch a wave.

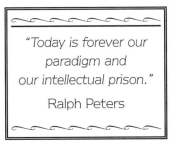

"Today is forever our paradigm and our intellectual prison."

Ralph Peters

Going from the beach to the stock market, the asset-allocation model of investment is only as good as its weakest link. If a particular allocation yields zero or negative returns, the entire portfolio suffers. Yes, you have minimized risk, but you accept mediocre results. There's no nice way of saying this: Averaging makes you . . . well, average. It is no surprise that most mutual funds, utilizing diversification, fail to beat the performance of the S&P 500.

Fortunately, there is an alternative. Contrast business as usual with the investment approach of Warren Buffett. Not only has this Harvard-reject *thrived* in the market's downturn, but he is also the world's most successful investor and, after Bill Gates, the richest man in the United States. His approach, called "focused investing," is directed at building winning portfolios, not minimizing losses through diversification. To this end, his number one and two rules for success are: Never lose money, and never forget rule number one.[29]

---

[29] *www.investopedia.com/university/greatest/warrenbuffett.asp.*

Much has been written about Buffett, but the most important point is not so much what he does—the whys and wherefores of his success—but what he *does not do*. Buffett wants to surf. He does not wait and stick with investment advice that over the long haul keeps nearly everyone off the board. Why settle for anything less? There is no profit to be found committing time, energy, effort and money to a poor or no-surf proposition. In short, if you're sitting at a beach called diversification or asset allocation (or any name for that matter) and the conditions stink year after year, *get up and get out of there.*

If getting up and going can remove us from poor surfing conditions, it is reasonable to ask, "Why do people put up with them?" Well, consider the following story. Three young novices are having lunch at a prepaid, all-inclusive ocean resort somewhere in the South Pacific. After a few bites, one says to his friends, "Hey man, this food tastes *terrible.*" The second, chasing what little is left on his plate with a fork, responds, "Yeah, and it's such small portions, too." The third nods in agreement with his two buddies and adds, "But dudes, we already paid for it, so we might as well eat it!"[30]

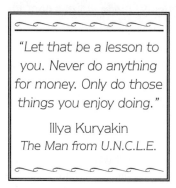

"Let that be a lesson to you. Never do anything for money. Only do those things you enjoy doing."

Illya Kuryakin
The Man from U.N.C.L.E.

Hilarious, right? The fancy term for explaining what's going on in this scenario is "the fallacy of sunken costs." If the food is bad, who cares how little or how much there is? Moreover, who in their right mind would eat something that tastes awful simply because one has already paid for it? It's irrational. When someone

---

[30] Adapted from the Woody Allen movie, *Annie Hall.*

is caught under the sway of sunken costs, however, his mind engages in singular acrobatics that keep him committed to poor surfing (or in this case, eating) conditions, wherever they may be.[31] Let's look at another example.

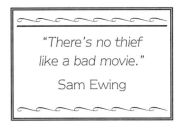

"There's no thief like a bad movie."

Sam Ewing

You're in college and on a very tight budget. With a few friends from the dorm, you go to a movie. You pay seven dollars for your ticket. After fifteen minutes, all the sane members of the audience, yourself included, are saying, "This movie is a dog. It's so bad, it barks! I can't believe it. What a waste of money." As you sit there fuming, however, the logic of sunken costs grabs hold. You rationalize, *Well, I've only watched fifteen minutes. Maybe it will get better.* Plus, you think, *I've already spent my seven bucks, so I might as well stick it out a little longer.*

At forty-five minutes you're still sitting there thinking the same thing. In addition, you've invested another thirty minutes of your time. Now, of course, the pressure is really on to hang in until the end. *I've*

---

[31] Dawes, R. *Rational Choice in an Uncertain World.* New York: Harcourt, Brace & Jovanovich, 1988.

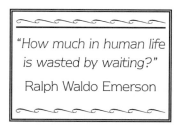

already watched most of it, you say to yourself, the sunken costs now firmly in control of your mind, *so I might as well see how it ends.*

No matter how reasonable this behavior may seem, it is completely and totally *irrational.* By choosing to stay at a bad movie *because* you've already paid for it and, then later on, *because* of the time you've already invested, you are saying, in effect, "I'd rather pay seven dollars to be miserable than be where I really want to be right now." That's not all. Once you choose to be miserable because you've already paid for it, you're also choosing to spend precious time pursuing known misery instead of other unknown opportunities.

Regardless of the results, the money and time you've already spent is already gone. It's sunk. And simply put, *sunken costs should not affect decisions about the future.* Yes, you're out the money, but so what? What's done is done. You remain free to move on to whatever you'd really rather be doing.

In sum, poor surfing conditions are found everywhere. The key consideration, however, is what you do about them. Sure, you can do nothing, waiting it out and hoping circumstances will improve. Sometimes that works, especially if poor turns into good in a short period. Continuing to wait because of all the time or money you've already invested in waiting or because you believe it will all average out in the end, is a strategy not likely to lead to the good life.

Wipeouts

Wipeout \'wIp-"aut \ *n* [origin: America, 1921] (1) What happens when the wave gets the best of you; (2) to fall off your board while riding a wave. *Synonyms:* blasted, drilled, bullwinkled, nailed, to eat foam, get rag-dolled, railed or pounded. *Antonym:* to not surf.

Danny Gans is something of a phenomenon.[32] For most of the last decade he's been voted "Las Vegas Entertainer of the Year"—a singular accomplishment. Like the song in the commercial says, "He's hot, hot, HOT!" In case you haven't heard of him, Gans is a singer-comedian-impressionist-actor. In his act, he not only captures the mannerisms of the celebrities he impersonates, but he manages to actually *look* and *sing* like them, morphing his face and voice into musicians as diverse as Michael Jackson and Willie Nelson. In some cases, he actually imitates two at a time, for instance, in a duet between the late Nat King Cole and daughter Natalie.

Praised by industry critics and appealing to all ages, he wows audiences time after time, packing them into an auditorium specially built for him at the luxurious Mirage hotel. Though not exhaustive, his other awards include: Headliner of the Year, Best All-Around Performer, Best Comedian, Best Male Las Vegan and Best Singer. Not surprisingly, his performances are sold out months in advance.

Despite his meteoric ride to the top in Vegas, Gans did not start as, nor even aspire to be, an entertainer. Rather, as a child, he dreamed of being the third baseman for the Los Angeles Dodgers. He worked hard at it throughout his adolescence, eventually being drafted by the Kansas City Royals when he was still in high school. As

---

[32] *www.dannygansshow.com/biography.htm.*

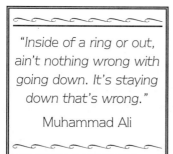

> *"Inside of a ring or out, ain't nothing wrong with going down. It's staying down that's wrong."*
>
> Muhammad Ali

luck would have it, however, he was forced to forgo this opportunity because of an injury. Later, while in college, he turned down yet another offer, this time from the Chicago White Sox. It just wasn't the right time.

Two years later, it looked as if his dream to play professional baseball would finally be realized. He was ready, mentally and physically. After signing, he was sent to play in the minor leagues. Once again, however, the fates were aligned against him. An injury to his Achilles tendon brought to a screeching halt a lifetime of aspirations. In surfing terms, Gans had experienced a wipeout—his third in as many times at bat. Barely up and riding, he'd been rocked from his board by forces beyond his control and sent to the bottom.

Ask any surfer. Wipeouts are an integral part of the sport. It's true. There's simply no way to avoid them. As long as you've checked bottom conditions before venturing out, most times it's a conk on the head by an errant board, a scrape along the ocean bottom or a lungful of seawater. Fortunately, death-by-wipeout is statistically rare.

> *"Mishaps are like knives that either serve us or cut us as we grasp them by the blade or the handle."*
>
> James Russell Lowell

Nonetheless, they can and do hurt and, if the wave is big enough, can also ruin your day. More troubling, when bad, they can seriously challenge your resolve to head back into the surf.

For his part, Gans paddled back out to the lineup and

popped up on the next wave to pass his way. Using his talents as a singer and comedian, this new ride carried him to a career in entertainment. For the next fifteen years, he traveled the corporate entertainment circuit, singing and doing stand-up comedy and impressions before stadium-sized crowds. It was a good ride. Audiences liked him, and he made a good living. At length, however, Gans began to feel that something was missing. Plus, the constant travel was taking a toll on his young family.

A pivotal moment occurred when he caught a performance by Sammy Davis Jr. Inspired by the master showman, Gans resolved to build himself a career in one location. Realizing that he could not catch this next wave until he'd bailed out of the one he was currently riding, he once again showed his surfer moxie and bravely walked away from the road. And the rest is, as they say, history. Not only did Gans find a permanent home for his family and talent on the Las

ONE DAY
I REALISED ALL
MY WIPEOUTS WERE
MY CHANCE TO WIPEOUT
EVERYTHING THAT
WAS HOLDING ME BACK!

Vegas strip, but his determination following a series of wipeouts led to a homerun in the income department. He has a ten-year, $150-million contract!

As the story of Danny Gans illustrates, life, like surfing, is a series of good rides interrupted by wipeouts or a series of wipeouts interrupted by good rides. The good life, it might even be said, can't be appreciated without the bad. In this regard, many have offered comment. Consider the following:

- "Sleep, riches and health, to be truly enjoyed, must be interrupted."—Jean Paul Fichter
- "Victory is sweetest when you have known defeat."—Malcolm Forbes
- "Misfortunes tell us what fortune is."—Thomas Fuller
- "He that can't endure the bad will not live to see the good."—Yiddish Proverb

> *"Your living is determined not so much by what life brings to you as by the attitude you bring to life; not so much by what happens to you as by the way your mind looks at what happens."*
>
> John Holmer Miller

So, whether heads or tails, up or down, sailing or smashed, it's usually the outlook rather than the wipeout itself that ultimately matters. Surfers say, "It's nothing personal. Getting creamed every now and then simply goes with the territory."

Overcoming obstacles and dealing with misfortune is the stuff of Hollywood films, TV newsmagazines and docudramas, and many novels. From the time of David and Goliath forward, we humans have shown a strong interest, an affinity even, for stories of survival and triumph. We like to root for the little guy. We want to see victory snatched from the jaws of defeat and believe that persistence and perseverance will, in the end, win the day. But there's a catch to this logic, a hook hidden in the cheese, so to speak, that can be deadly to anyone who takes the bait.

Scientists have actually found that people who personalize wipeouts—that is, who believe they are the cause or source of their own misfortune—actually increase the risk of having more wipeouts. In contrast to prevailing self-help and cultural wisdom—identify your shortcomings and take responsibility for fixing them—those who study such matters have actually found that people who blame an unfortunate event or even a series of wipeouts on external factors (the weather, having a bad day, and the like), get back on track more quickly than those who hold themselves responsible!

In a series of studies, researchers examined how sports teams explained a bad performance or even a slump.[33] Two distinct styles emerged. In one, losses were attributed to external factors: the fans,

---

[33] Seligman, M.E.P. *Learned Optimism*. New York: Knopf, 1981.

the venue, the noise and the day of the week. In the other, teams assumed personal responsibility for the loss: They played terribly, didn't work together, botched every opportunity, or left their skills, brains and brawn on the sidelines. In contrast to what you might expect, the results were clear. Teams that adopted the "take responsibility for our mistakes" perspective fared far worse the following season than those who blamed outside forces.

Filmmaker and perennial neurotic Woody Allen once observed, "Eighty percent of success is showing up." In contrast, your average surfers know that at least eighty percent of the good life is showing *back* up following a wipeout. As much as we hate admitting it, there is a great deal of truth to the old bumper sticker, "S@%t happens!" It's nothing personal. So, if you can, paddle back out to the line-up and look for the next incoming set of waves.

On the other hand, maybe you're tired, had enough for the day. You're ready to get out of the water and head back home. Surfers do, after all, have a life outside of surfing. What do they do when they're not riding the ocean waves? Turn the page and find out.

6

Where the Surf Meets the Turf (What Surfers Do When They're Not Surfing)

Live while you live ... and seize
the pleasures of the present day.

Philip Doddridge

With all this talk about making your way in the waves, it's easy to forget that we spend the vast majority of our time living on land. We're no amphibians—that's why Aquaman is considered a superhero, right? Maybe the surf is flat, maybe it's huge and blown out, or maybe you're hanging out in the city, mountains, desert or some other place far away from the beach.

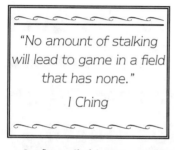

"No amount of stalking will lead to game in a field that has none."

I Ching

Surfmaster says, "If there are waves, then hang ten. If there are no waves, do something else." As much as we'd all like to be on a permanent surfin' safari, life certainly doesn't end where the surf meets the turf. In fact, this is where it begins. . . .

Surfing sailed into pop culture in the 1950s, making its way into the movies and magazines and eventually the shopping malls. There was only one problem with all the enthusiasm for the new water sport: The vast majority of people did not live near the seashore. No matter how interested or mesmerized a person might be, no waves were to be found in such far-flung places as Lubbock, Texas, Fort Wayne, Indiana, or Green Bay, Wisconsin. What to do? That's where skateboarding enters the picture. The enthusiastic originators of what, not coincidentally, came to be called "sidewalk surfing" were simply trying to "bring the beach within reach."

There was a learning curve, of course. The first skateboards were, at best, a product of folk engineering. In most instances, metal wheels were yanked off rusting shoe skates lying unused in old garages and then fastened with nails to a wooden board—not a very smooth ride, to say the least. Next came clay wheels. And while these managed to iron out some of the bumps in the road, they were still a pretty rough ride. Think Flintstones here. It was less "Yabba dabba do," and more "dabba dud."

Then, in 1970, a surfer by the name of Frank Nasworthy stumbled upon a plastic manufacturing factory in Pucellville, Virginia—a town not on any map of hot surf spots, by the way. The company was making urethane wheels for a new generation of roller skates. Amidst the strong aroma of plastic, Frank immediately smelled the potential for skateboarding. By 1973, his Cadillac Wheels had pushed the new activity to a higher level. Finally, the smoothness of surfing had been brought to the streets of suburbia.[34]

The skateboard saga continues. Ever heard of the Z-Boys? This team of young surfers had a problem. In order to catch the best waves at their favorite pier near Venice, California, they had to be out in the water very early. In and of itself, this wasn't a problem. Surfers are notoriously early risers, beating a path to the beach long before the crowds arrive and the tourists become impossible to dodge in the water.

The real problem was that no matter the time they arrived, the surf near the Dogtown pier was generally blown out by late morning. As a result, the committed group of wave riders was left with nothing else to do for the rest of the day. Not ones to wait around for the surf to come back up, the boys began scouring the streets.

As fate or luck (depending on your point of view) would have it, all the private swimming pools in the Los Angeles area had been drained because of a serious drought in southern California. The Z-Boys became the first to go vertical, zipping up and down the banked walls of empty pools, unleashing their surf-style moves on the waves of concrete.[35] Bottom line? By seeing and taking advantage

[34] Brooke, M. *The Concrete Wave: The History of Skateboarding.* Woodside, Calif.: Warwick Publishing, 1999.
[35] *Dogtown and Z-Boys.* Vans Off the Wall Productions. Director: Stacy Peralta. Producer Agi Orsi, 2002.

of the opportunities in their own neighborhood, the troupe had discovered a way to do what they loved virtually anytime they wanted.

Finally, consider the SeaGaia Ocean Dome complex in Miyazaki, Japan. Turning the planet into someone's version of paradise has been the subject of many science-fiction novels. In this case, fact is stranger than fiction. The complex houses an artificial surfer's paradise so close to the real thing that it's almost surreal. This man-made lagoon features a wave-making machine that can crank out ten-foot surf and even a barrel here and there for those who like to shoot the tube. There is a sloping bottom, matching the topography of a natural beach, and a painted sky with clouds in the background, providing the illusion that one is actually surfing outdoors.[36]

It would be hard to come up with any more literal examples than these of trying to bring the beach within reach. Of course, there's a limit to such artifices. Strangely enough, that limitation is not in the way that these pseudo-surfing experiences fall *short* of replicating the real thing. Although it may seem counter-intuitive, their actual limitation lies in how *closely* they resemble it.

---

[36] Brisbick, J. "When Chlorine Comes into the Picture." *Big,* Volume 43, 2002.

Now, at this point, you may rightly wonder, "Isn't the definition of a good example something that is like what it is trying to represent?" And you'd be right . . . at least at one level. At another level, however, such thinking misses the point entirely.

Sure, you *could* skateboard whenever the waves are flat to continually hone your balance, and yes, you can surf every day in the indoor, artificial perfection of the SeaGaia complex, even changing the wave size and form to meet varying real-world conditions. Wait a few years, and the imagineers at Disney will probably build a *Star Trek*–like holodeck so real that anyone living anywhere can try out the sport. And maybe, just maybe, practicing long enough in any one of these current or future settings may help a person get good enough to tour on the professional circuit. Yet no matter how close such experiences are to the real thing, no matter how faithfully they represent reality, they are still not surfing.

In many ways, we live in an increasingly virtual world, separated from rather than connected to life by our experiences. To wit, digital communication via e-mail, cell phones and videoconferencing has replaced face-to-face conversation. In many offices, for example, it is

standard practice to send an e-mail to a coworker even though that person may be sitting in an adjoining cubicle!

Meanwhile, the television has become a fully integrated member of the family in many homes, with Katie, Matt and Al as much a part of breakfast time together as Mom, Dad and the kids (sometimes more). Speaking of television, when a woman standing outside the Paris hotel in Las Vegas was asked by a local newscaster what she liked about the city, she replied, "I love it . . ." and then, pointing to the near-full-size replica of the Eiffel Tower in the background, added, "Now I don't need to fly all that way to visit France."

In order to forestall any potential misunderstanding, let us be perfectly clear. We are *not* saying that our modern world actually *causes* people to mistake ruse for reality. Clearly, the woman visiting Vegas *knew* she was in Vegas and not Paris. And surely, the families noted above are aware that the cast members of the *Today Show* are not *really* a part of their family. It is just that in an increasing number of instances, what's real doesn't matter much. For a variety of reasons (time pressures, money, number of commitments, etc.), virtual experiences are deemed good enough.

You have to admit, it is easier and, let's face it, more efficient than

IT'S IMPORTANT TO KEEP A FIRM GRIP ON REALITY... AND IF YOU CAN'T AT LEAST FAKE ONE

having to "fly all that way" to France or count on your family members to be as cheerful and engaging every morning as "America's First Family." But therein lies the hook. In spite of a diet rich in images and saturated experience, many of us leave the table hungering for something more. Starved for meaning and fulfillment, we end up back at the trough rooting around for some experience to fill the void—a pattern that has led to the sad and cynical expression of the era, "been there, done that."

In response, surfers say, "You may have done it, but you were never really there." Sure, cruising on a concrete curl or catching a tube in an artificial wave pool can be a pretty good substitute for the real thing on a day when you can't make it to the beach. Such examples show how something deeply satisfying and meaningful, like surfing, can be brought into other experiences and environments through the hands and minds of a complex and technologically advanced species. But they are still replicas of something more genuine, more authentic. Confuse the two and you miss out on feeling the sand between your toes, watching the seagulls swoop and the dolphins leap, smelling the salty sea air and coconut suntan oil. In short, you'll miss the whole experience of surfing.

Watch surfers for a while and you'll quickly notice that most of their time is *not* spent peeling down the face of a wave, but

> "A surfer in the tube is the epitome of 'be here now.' The roof of the tube being the 'now,' the future immediately ahead and constantly erasing itself as we race along under the curtain, our past, the wake disappearing into the foam behind us."
>
> Timothy Leary

rather enjoying the lull *between* the sets of waves, paddling around in the water, shooting the breeze with their buds, and lounging around and bagging some rays. The lesson is clear: If you've only come for the *sensation* associated with riding, you'll probably find the *experience* of surfing a cold, exhausting and lonely affair. Ignore this, and you might be a "pro," but never a "bro." More than likely, you'll just give up, paddle back into shore, and seek that sense of meaning and fulfillment elsewhere.

Surfing, as we have experienced it and tried to convey in these pages, is more a way of living—an attitude or mindset—than a sport or leisure activity. When casting about on life's uncertain waters, it advises us to look for and take advantage of breaking opportunities. On land and between sets, it encourages us to see and experience the richness in the ordinary, the magic in the mundane, the sacred in the simple and the beauty even in the broken.

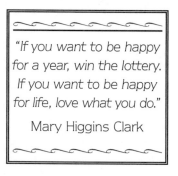

"If you want to be happy for a year, win the lottery. If you want to be happy for life, love what you do."

Mary Higgins Clark

How, exactly, is one to gain such perspective? Well, hopefully, six chapters into the book, we've managed to fashion a set of surfing lenses that sharpens the focus to some degree. The rest comes down to practice, consciously and purposefully taking the time to touch, taste, smell, see and hear, to be fully immersed in the present moment—whether lying on your back watching the clouds pass overhead, washing the dishes, changing your baby's diaper, or simply breathing deeply in and out (do not try the latter while changing the baby's diaper).

The attitude that we're talking about is captured in the following story. Two gremmies were talking while waxing their boards in preparation for the morning's surf. One boasted to the other, "Dude, I'm learning to surf from the ace of all aces. He never gets caught inside, goes aerial on every wave and can do a 360 with his eyes closed." The other, demonstrating his superior grasp of surfing, simply replied, "My teacher is also a master surfer. When he's tired, he sleeps. When he's hungry, he eats. When the surf is flat, he runs along the shore, and in between sets of waves, he talks to other surfers."

We'll be the first to admit that being present—that is, connected to our lives as they unfold in the moment—is no easy task. We often find our minds wandering, fantasizing about something else we'd rather be

> "Of all the will toward the ideal in mankind, only a small part can manifest itself in public action. All the rest must be content with small and obscure deeds. The sum of these, however, is a thousand times stronger than the acts of those who receive wide public attention. The latter, compared to the former, are like the foam on the waves of a deep ocean."
>
> Albert Schweitzer

doing. Nowhere is this truer than in the basic activities hinted at in the story above: eating a balanced diet, getting enough physical exercise and sleep, and connecting with and nurturing our closest relationships.

Consider the following factoids:

- Although there is no shortage of food in the United States, many Americans suffer health problems resulting from poor nutrition (eating foods that contain empty calories, lacking the vitamins, minerals, proteins, beneficial fatty acids and other nutrients necessary to promote optimal health). Far from benign, such dietary habits are linked to heart disease and cancer, two of the biggest killers of our time.[37]

- Although studies have continually shown that sleep is a restorative process, helping to repair the body as well as enhance energy, memory and immunity to illness, a recent survey found that over the last five years people in the United States are working more and sleeping less. Indeed, 63 percent of adults get less than the recommended amount per night. As a result, 40 percent report having trouble staying awake during the day![38]

- Although experts have agreed for years that even a small amount

---

[37] National Institute of Diabetes & Digestive & Kidney Diseases of the National Institutes of Health Web site, *www.niddk.nih.gov*.

[38] National Sleep Foundation Web site. "2002 'Sleep in America' Pool": *www.sleepfoundation.org*. Report prepared for release March 2002.

of physical activity per week —as little as half an hour of uninterrupted walking, for example—has a measurable impact on prevention of disease, quality of life and longevity, Americans are as a group increasingly sedentary in their daily routine. Meanwhile, we're eating antide-

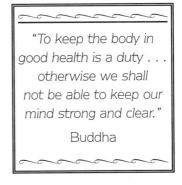

"To keep the body in good health is a duty . . . otherwise we shall not be able to keep our mind strong and clear."

Buddha

pressants like they're going out of season—even though recent research has actually shown that exercise causes the release of neurotransmitters in the brain related to a positive mood and general sense of well-being.[39]

- Although an abundance of research shows that people in committed, long-term relationships, as well as those with a strong social support network (friends, extended family), feel happier and actually live longer, more adults are living alone and away from family and close friends than ever before in the history of the country. At the same time, the divorce rate continues to hover around 50 percent. By the way, people who enjoy committed relationships also have more sex. And what could be wrong with that?

And finally:

- A growing body of evidence is finding that people with a strong spiritual practice (regular church attendance, meditation, prayer) are happier, better adjusted, and yes, healthier. This finding is true, by the way, regardless of the particular spiritual path chosen (religion or denomination). And yet, while surveys

---

[39] Statistics Related to Overweight and Obesity, *www.niddk.nih.gov/health/nutrit/pubs/statobes.htm.* December 2002.

consistently find that 95 percent of Americans believe in some form of higher power, the majority of them do not engage in any regular or formal practice of their beliefs outside times of crisis.

To be sure, we're not suggesting that you become a muscle-bound gym rat, take up sleeping-in as a hobby, buy a health-food store, stay in an unhappy (yet committed) relationship, or even run off and join a religious commune. Not that there's anything wrong with any of these choices, mind you. They just miss the point: It's much easier to end up floundering around in the froth and foam near the shore when these fundamental aspects of life are out of balance.

In many ways, the modern world actively conspires against attending to these basic building blocks of daily life. The comforts and conveniences most of us enjoy simultaneously enable us to forgo thinking altogether about the tasks that, one generation prior to our own, absorbed the bulk of people's time, attention and effort. Do technological advances and falling literacy rates portend a future in which the government and media point to the paunchiness of our brains instead of, as they do now, our behinds? As crazy as it might sound, most people alive a century ago would find our high-tech gyms—with their rows of exercise machines and mirror-bound, surround-sound-equipped aerobic rooms—difficult to fathom. After all, they didn't need to set aside time or go to a specially designed place to exercise. Physical activity was inher-

> "Life can be found only in the present moment. The past is gone, the future is not yet here, and if we do not go back to ourselves in the present moment, we cannot be in touch with life."
>
> Thich Nhat Hanh

ent in their day-to-day routine. And therein lies the key: *Make such activities a part of life rather than one more thing apart from everything else in life you have to do.*

Surfers say, "Enough said, dude. We get the point." Paraphrasing the thirty-third president of the United States, Harry Truman, we say, "The book stops here." We hope you enjoyed the ride. As for ourselves, we're off to bag some rays and catch a few waves. Hopefully, at this point, you are, too. Be sure and leave the book behind before you head out. You don't need it weighing you down. Anyway, it would just get all wet and soggy. Plus, you'll need your hands free in order to experience everything the surf on your turf has to offer.

Glossary of Surfing Terms

360	A maneuver in which the board (and rider) spins 360 degrees on the face of the wave.
Aerial	Part of a maneuver in which the surfer and his/her board leaves the water. This maneuver requires split-second timing and is only performed by expert surfers.
Caught Inside	Having great trouble paddling back out because the incoming waves are too big, powerful, difficult or impossible to get beyond.
Cut Out	To exit a wave.
Gremmie	Beginning surfer.
Grommet	An adolescent or young surfer.
Kick Out	See Cut Out.
Line Up	The point where the waves break for the first time.
Poser	A person who doesn't surf, but says he does.

Soup　　　　　The white-washy water located in the impact zone, frothy and full of bubbles.

Surfz Up!　　　Waves are breaking and surf-able; I'm out of here!

Trimming　　　Continually adjusting your position on the board so it planes and achieves its maximum speed given the way the wave is unfolding.

Wannabe　　　See Poser.

About the Authors

Scott Miller was a long way from his sunny Southern California origins when he was finally rediscovered. In spite of years of attention and therapy, he was still an enigma to the kindhearted people who'd taken him in and cared for him in the small Midwestern town. They weren't even sure of his name. For some unknown reason, his voice had been silenced. The only clue to his identity was a single word, uttered every once in a while, either in his sleep or while eating a meal: "Roseboard." His caretakers tried in vain for many years to trace the meaning of this enigmatic expression. Eventually, however, they gave up trying to understand the young man they'd found wandering the snowy winter streets of the tiny landlocked village, clad in little more than flip-flops and a swimsuit. "Enough!" they said. "Goldilocks," as members of the community took to calling him on account of his long, curly blond hair, "is simply going to be our responsibility." And from that time forward, each person living in the town took a turn taking care of Scott.

Sometimes it seemed as if the homes in which he stayed and beds on which he slept were too small. At other times, they seemed too big. Never did things seem just right. Then one day, a young businessman seated in a nearby booth at the local diner overheard Scott mumbling, "Roseboard." Locals immediately knew the man was from out of town when he jumped up from his seat and, forgoing any conversational formalities, immediately caught Scott's eye and asked,

"You know about *Roseboard?* The all-time best surfboard ever made? You from Southern Cal?" And at that point, the lights came on for Scott. "Yes," Scott said, "I *am.*" And then, in front of the tanned stranger and all the townspeople at the diner that day, Scott recounted his life story up to the time of his disappearance.

He'd grown up a surfer but had lost his sense of purpose and self when his career path had steered him away from the beach he so loved. Little more need be said. He thanked the members of the small town for their years of devotion and care. The life and happiness they witnessed in him as he prepared to leave led a number of them to suggest he write a book about his experience.

Long drawn to paleontology, **Mark Hubble** spent many years digging in Colorado, Montana, New Mexico and Arizona. His ambition was to discover the "reference predator"—the dinosaur that would set the benchmark for ferocity and aggressiveness. As any vertebrate paleontologist will tell you, of course, this is extremely hard work. For one who grew up on the lush and wet East Coast, the experience eventually proved too much. Therefore, Mark, having spent far too much time dehydrated in the badlands, decided to forgo the digging and concoct a creature with an assortment of disarticulated bones he had collected. After several weeks closed away in an abandoned barn—gluing and screwing the beast together—he called a news conference announcing the discovery of "Bigandmeanasaurus"—the biggest and meanest dinosaur ever found. When reporters arrived and inspected the find, however, their immediate comment was, "Well, it's not that big," followed by, "It looks like a French poodle on stilts." One journalist added, "Actually pretty damn silly looking if you ask me. Is this thing real?" Mark knew the gig was up and hoofed it over to the desert as fast as his legs could carry him.

Running, then walking, then crawling, he finally collapsed. What happened next, he is still hard-pressed to relate coherently, but suffice it to say he had an epiphany, a sublime peek into the workings of the universe. In this moment of clarity, he decided he needed water and lots of it. He stood up, fell over an ancient lava flow and landed smack dab on an interstate, pointing West. A compassionate trucker named Ishmael, carting coffins to California, took pity and conveyed the wretch to Malibu. Awakened by the possibilities of so much water, Mark self-published a card-table book on the ocean and surfing, particularly women surfers. Full of himself and enthusiasm, he hit the road to promote his product, and by happenstance wound up in a small backwater town in the Midwest. Here he unexpectedly encountered a blond-haired fellow with a special knowledge of Roseboard surfboards. After extended discussions and hairsplitting negotiations, Mark saw in this man a future business partner. After all, water is water and kindred souls are hard to find. A new venture was born. They decided to write a book together.

Before adopting the principles of surfing wisdom found in this book and applying them successfully to his life, **Seth Houdeshell** was working a dead-end job and hanging out with dead-beat friends. Everything he saw seemed to be some shade of gray, and food had lost its taste. His only accomplishment was a new method he invented for organizing his sock and underwear drawer that was based loosely on the Dewey Decimal System. This was curious, considering that all of his socks and underwear were the same color and brand. The only shadow of pleasure in his dim life came from compulsively pinching and popping the air pockets in plastic bubble wrap. This was causing some occupational difficulty as the callus he developed on his thumb and forefinger prevented him from holding a pen or using a keyboard. After getting arrested for disturbing the peace at a local mail center and packaging supply store, he decided it was time to turn over a new leaf and break out of his old comfortable patterns of behavior.

Then, while cleaning the elephant trailer—his job while on tour with a traveling circus—he found new hope in the shell of a peanut he had swept up. He saw within it the face and body of Elvis, but then turned it slightly, and Leonard Nimoy appeared. He picked up another from the floor—Bob Barker—and yet another—Olivia Newton-John. It was not long before Seth realized where the waves were really breaking. He started production from his home, creating tiny shoebox scenes from American history and cinema out of peanut pods that were painted to resemble famous personages. His company is cleverly called Shoebox Peanut People. These have become collector's items and sell for hundreds of dollars apiece on eBay. Good things really do come in small packages!

Seth has now stopped working himself, but continues to direct a team of artisans who bring his ideas to life. His ample free time is mostly spent in leisure with his supermodel wife, sailing the South Pacific on his private yacht. He has been granted honorary citizenship in several countries on four different continents, and one of his shoebox peanut people scenes commemorating Neil Armstrong's first walk on the moon will be sent into orbit by NASA this coming year.

John Byrne was a mild-mannered art student until the fateful day he was bitten by a radioactive cartoonist and discovered that he had been given amazing cartoon powers. Becoming Born Again in 2000, thanks to the ministry of Disco Diva Candi Staton, means that he now uses his powers for good (and can legitimately gain access to the gates of heaven by claiming "I'm with the band").

One day while out surfing near the circle of Carey, a tidal wave propelled him all the way to Malibu. Scott, Mark and Seth were immediately impressed with his moves, both on the wave as well as on the cartoon pad he held in his hands. When they asked him how he'd managed to stay on top and keep the sand out of his pants on such a long journey, John used his magic marker to draw cartoon beards on the three.

Feeling like they'd found their long-lost (and humorous) brother, Scott, Mark and Seth asked John to do the cartoons for their surfing book. This is John's first attempt at combining cartooning with surfing. He claims it has been a liberating experience, although the paper has been getting extremely soggy.

Really, About the Authors . . .

Scott D. Miller, Ph.D., grew up in sunny southern California, surfing the waves at Newport Beach. He is currently the codirector of the Institute for the Study of Therapeutic Change, where he works as a consultant helping individuals, organizations and businesses manage change and increase productivity. He is the author of many papers and coauthor of seven books including: *The Heroic Client, The Heart & Soul of Change, Escape from Babel* and *The Miracle Method: A Radically New Approach to Problem Drinking.*

Mark A. Hubble, Ph.D., grew up near Baltimore, Maryland, body-surfing the cold waters of the Atlantic. Presently, he works as a psychologist and national consultant. An accomplished writer and editor, Dr. Hubble has published numerous articles and is coauthor of *The Heart & Soul of Change, Escape from Babel, Psychotherapy with "Impossible" Cases* and *The Handbook of Solution-Focused Brief Therapy.*

Seth Houdeshell, L.M.S.W., is a licensed social worker, working and living in Austin, Texas, and surfing whenever and wherever he can. He received his bachelor's degree in psychology at Trinity University in San Antonio, Texas, and earned his master's degree in social work from the University of Texas at Austin.

John Byrne, originally from Dublin, Ireland, is one of Britain's top cartoonists, comedy writers and stand-up comedians with wide-ranging experience in performance, production and the teaching of creative skills. He is currently the resident artist on Nickelodeon TV (UK), drawing live and unscripted, and often with "art materials" that include everything from sausages to toothbrushes to TV presenters with luminous paint in their hair. He has a six-year-old son Pearse, is married to Fumi, and has a house full of teen in-laws (who he loves dearly—especially since realizing the importance of babysitters!).

All of the authors can be reached at *info@talkingcure.com.*

Change Your Life

It's not always easy to make a Big Decision, whether it's about marriage, education, career, kids, health, business or personal finances. *Get Off the Fence!* shows you how to make the decisions that count.

Code #0510 • Paperback • $12.95

In *Winning with One-Liners*, Pat Williams, one of the nation's premier speakers, has compiled an A-to-Z list of quick quips to make your presentations outstanding.

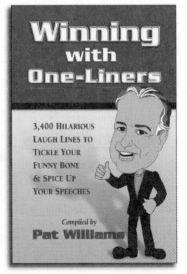

Code #057X • Paperback • $12.95

Available wherever books are sold.
To order direct: Phone 800.441.5569 • Online www.hcibooks.com
Prices do not include shipping and handling. Your response code is BKS.

All in a Day's Work

#1 New York Times & USA Today
BESTSELLING AUTHORS
Jack Canfield
Mark Victor Hansen
Maida Rogerson, Martin Rutte
& Tim Clauss

Chicken Soup Soup for the Soul® at Work

101 Stories of Courage, Compassion and Creativity in the Workplace

Code #424X • Paperback • $12.95

Chicken Soup for the Soul at Work gives you new options, new ways to succeed and, above all, a new love and appreciation for yourself, your job and those around you.

Whether you manage a staff of fifty or choreograph the comings and goings of a family of five, you are the ultimate multitasker. Chicken Soup for the Working Women's Soul celebrates the diversity and special contributions of women in the world of work.

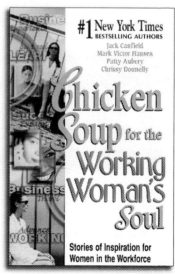

#1 New York Times
BESTSELLING AUTHORS
Jack Canfield
Mark Victor Hansen
Patty Aubery
Chrissy Donnelly

Chicken Soup for the Working Woman's Soul

Stories of Inspiration for Women in the Workforce

Code #0448 • Paperback • $12.95

The Power of Positive Thinking

Change Almost Anything in 21 Days provides both the inspiration and motivation needed to make important changes—from careers and relationships to parenting and health.

Code #0677 • Paperback • $12.95

Code #0995 • Paperback • $10.95

The wisdom this book offers will help you discover how to better understand yourself and find fulfillment by being who you are.